The Aesthetics of Ambiguity
Understanding and Addressing Monoculture

Pascal Gielen &
Nav Haq (eds.)

Antennae-Arts in Society
Valiz, Amsterdam

The Aesthetics of Ambiguity
Understanding and Addressing Monoculture

Pascal Gielen & Nav Haq (eds.)

Contributors

Paolo S.H. Favero
Pascal Gielen
Christine Greiner
Max Haiven
Nav Haq
Hedwig Houben
Iman Issa
Bojana Piškur
Public Movement
Jonas Staal
Mi You
Tirdad Zolghadr

Contents

Introduction
Ambiguity and Monocultures

Pascal Gielen &
Nav Haq

We start with a simple statement of 'relations'. What we understand as 'multiculturalism' might be defined in relation to 'monoculturalism'. This is the peculiar paradox and complexity that we wish to explore in this book. Anyone who feels integrated in a society and feels at home in their culture tends to be more easily open to the Other. On the other hand, those who feel that their identity and their 'own' culture are threatened will argue for multiculturalism much less easily. We might identify this as a general social tendency. Multiculturalism and pluralism presuppose a shared culture with shared values and convictions on such things as openness, democracy, equality, and cohabitation. Thus, if we understand 'monoculture' as being the homogeneous expression of a social or ethnic group, we see that the multicultural society is paradoxically built on monocultural convictions. And so, as we analyze in this book, both monocultures and multicultures find it very difficult to deal with real ambiguity. Rather, they only relate to what they feel mirrors themselves, instead of acknowledging that they are intrinsically connected.

As we write this introduction, statues and monuments are being brought down everywhere in the Global North and history is being challenged once again. As the cliché goes, history repeats itself, but the fact that it happens again suggests that the multicultural consensus was actually never a consensus. In short, the Black Lives Matter movement reaffirms 'our' monocultural perspective on multiculturalism and what suppresses it. But tearing down an image also reminds us how charged art can become at certain moments. No matter how idiosyncratic the artist's mind is, his or her work always shows the traces of a community, its history and indeed a culture. Or rather, it is only when an artefact manages to register in such a social fabric, when it stirs it, that it becomes a work of art. Art simply does not exist without that social dimension, without shared cultural references, yes, not without a 'we' who interpret, understand and appreciate differently than a 'they'. As French cultural sociologist Pierre Bourdieu pointed out as early as the 1980s (Bourdieu, 1984), art also always serves to distinguish us from the rest, not to identify with *that* culture but with *this* culture; to relate us to *this* and not *that* identity. In other words, art operates as both a reconciler and a divider within a community.

This dual role shows us that a society has always been ambiguous, possessing different characteristics simultaneously, and that the images and monuments that emerge from it are always a simplification. However, that ambiguity is now denied both by those who straighten statues and those who demolish those monuments; by those who verticalize, hierarchize and canonize, and those who think they can 'equalize' and 'horizontalize' the world completely. Both movements are equally 'monomaniacal', because both camps represent the world in black-and-white and displace all shades that flourish between them. It is as if in the heat of battle, they forget the colour palette of their own lives and the world around them. In short, both severely lack nuance. While the 'verticals' forget that their culture and symbols are not everyone's, those who strive for radical equality also forget that they make discriminatory moves. After all, dreaming and striving for more justice, or simply justice, places the focus on limited facets of the social fabric at the expense of others, and in the process, render identities as one-dimensional common denominators. Each side of this false dichotomy indicates that they find 'this' more important, valuable and meaningful than 'that', and so they want to fight for 'this' and not for 'that'. In other words, all iconoclasts have a different statue in mind that they want to pull down and replace with one they, want to identify with. And that vertical or horizontal movement always entails exclusion, of the values that one does not endorse or appreciate, and discards them with or without violence. These are the intolerant sides of vertical and horizontal monocultures. They simply do not acknowledge their relations to each other. Or in fact any other modes of living outside their own, whether existing or possible. However, art has historically also played a completely different role. Being able to deal with ambiguities, differences, and paradoxes is the outcome of a learning process and thus of cultivation, in which art has played a pivotal role since modernity. Modern and contemporary artists have constantly played with ambiguities, boundaries, and crossovers. Many artists have made it their prime occupation to bring ambiguities to the surface. Explaining the contradictions and paradoxes in a culture, reconciling what cannot be reconciled according to custom and routine—that's what contemporary artists are trained for and have become good at. The contemporary artist is a bricoleur, shaman, and charlatan who prepares peculiar blends and shakes indigestible cocktails. This, at least in the Global North, has been the ultimate mission of the artist since the nineteenth century. Often an artist has to play with cultural conventions to even be considered an 'artist'. Not always tolerated for their exploration of ambiguity—if we think about the case of avant-garde art being designated 'Entartete Kunst' under the Third Reich, for example—artists have challenged dominant or imposed conceptions of culture, from Nazi Art, Socialist Realism or other forms of official state art, to the influence of liberal capitalism.

Many studies now assume that there is a correlation, but no proven causality thus far, between dealing with ambiguity in perception and encounters in everyday life—such as for example encountering those of ambiguous race, gender, or sexuality. In other words, those who are open to ambiguous or paradoxical stimuli would also be more open to the Other, whether the Other in themselves or in society. In contrast, those who find ambiguous experiences and encounters something to be afraid of, possess similar sentiments towards Otherness. We consider the pioneering work of psychoanalyst Else Frenkel-Brunswik following the Second World War, who analyzed ethnocentricity as part of her research into the authoritarian personality through her ideas of 'Ambiguity Tolerance-Intolerance'. She discovered such direct relations between perception, cognitive function, and social outlook (Frenkel-Brunswik 1949). Thus, her work can be valuable when brought into the realm of art and visual culture. It can bring positive insights into the effects of our relations with ambiguous things such as art, and particularly in the context of monoculture. Both Nav Haq and Pascal Gielen refer to her work in their contributions to this book.

A positive scientific connection between an appreciation of contemporary art and a cross-cultural attitude might therefore also be assumed. However, those who like to engage with ambiguities within the walls of a museum, do not necessarily do so outside of those walls, in the 'real world'. After all, the interaction with the rules of art is itself based on a monoculture, mainly that of an educated middle class. At least a part of that social class feels comfortable with the strange and the ambiguous, as long as these stay safely within the walls of the imaginary and fiction. In other words, playing with the rules of art is tolerated, but playing with the imminent rules of a society or culture at large isn't, yet. Perhaps that is why artists who feel called upon to intervene in society or in public space, but invoke the game with the rules of contemporary art, often fail. The actions they undertake and the works they make start from a monoculture of openness and novelty, which is rarely understood in the outside world. The current work of art in public space therefore is met with incomprehension, sometimes aggression, but mostly with total indifference. This game with the rules of art is simply not understood because it is not a subtle game with the cultural conventions that people know and experience daily. It is in the 'wrong' place. Until of course events and contexts make them a point of contention, in which case any signs of ambiguity are denied.

With this book, we have looked for artists, thinkers, and institutional practices that are navigating this border, who dare to play with the rules of a broader society and thus generate ambiguity 'at large'. In other words, we investigate how dealing with ambiguous stimuli can also spread into the wider world. We portray art and artists who adopt ambiguity and paradoxes outside the laboratory of fiction, and perhaps also risk their own familiar monoculture in doing so. More specifically, we want to see where the game with artistic conventions can become a game with broader cultural conventions in society at large. How can familiarity with ambiguous images, experiences and other stimuli lead to familiarity and tolerance of the ambiguities in ourselves and the society around us? What do we mean by 'ambiguity'? What strategies do artists develop who navigate at the liminal zone between artistic and cultural or social conventions? How do they make their familiar monoculture the basis of understanding and learning to live within societies that are complex and always ambiguous? What works and what does not? Can the aesthetics of ambiguity help define a future *modus operandi* for art institutions? In this book, we consider those strategies and practices between art and society, including their successes and failures.

The Aesthetics of Ambiguity also deals with the ambivalence of identity politics. Identity politics often uses monocultural principles to claim the rights of a specific constituency of identity—race, gender, and sexuality being the most visible ones, historically-speaking. In this struggle for emancipation, specific cultural characteristics are often highlighted while others are suppressed or disguised. In such a discursive strategy, cultural ambiguity dissolves, so that identity policy decays and hardens into ghetto-ization or ontological 'purism'. From that moment on, the emancipation struggle turned, for example, into 'anti-racist racism' (Sartre on *Négritude*) or die-hard ethno-nationalism. In this book, we also examine how artists, curators, researchers, and theorists across various disciplines deal with the point at which the heterodox struggle for certain rights turns into an orthodox confirmation and convulsive defence of consolidated positions. The underlying question here is: is emancipation and the pursuit of equal rights possible without an identity-based reflex? The well-known traditional Marxist answer to this question is 'yes, by taking economic inequality as the starting point'. But does such a struggle not presuppose that a 'Klasse an sich' becomes a 'Klasse für sich', and thus assumes an identity through class consciousness? Is there, besides identity politics, no possibility of emancipation in the space of ambiguity? Could such a thing as 'ambiguity politics' be possible? As indicated earlier, it appears that an 'aesthetics of ambiguity' resonates in the contemporary art world. Again, in this book, we want to map this, and give the word to artists and thinkers who test out such strategies of ambiguity, including outside the game of art, and thus engage with the field of politics and society at large.

We briefly introduce our contributors. Firstly, inspired by Antonio Gramsci, sociologist Pascal Gielen defines the last decade as one of 'organic crisis'. In such periods many (economic, political, ecological) crises follow each other while the hegemonic order cannot deal with them anymore in a convincing way, and a new political paradigm that can sufficiently deal with them is not yet invented. Ambiguity aesthetics can inspire a kind of ambiguity politics that could deal with the problems and contradictions of this contemporary world of rambling causalities in a better way, according to Gielen.

Nav Haq takes a closer look at art, and considers the historical trajectory of modern and contemporary art in relation to monoculturalism in society, including the increasing tendency of ethnocentric nationalism. Using Frenkel-Brunswik's ideas of Ambiguity Tolerance-Intolerance as a basis, he considers whether art (both aesthetically and ontologically speaking) and institutional practices, can create a long-term sphere of influence for society at large in helping us to discover new liberalisms.

For several years, artist Jonas Staal has undertaken research into propaganda. His essay analyzes the historical exhibitions organized by the Nazis, including the infamous *Entartete Kunst* exhibition of 1937, and considers how they were part of the Nazi propaganda machine. Staal suggests that the designation

'Entartete Kunst' remains in operation within exhibition practices, including in reverse form. Using the example of the Freethinkers' Space in the Dutch parliament, where the 'freedom of expression' reasoning was mobilized to suggest that left-wing elites repress cultural expression to appease an Islamic immigrant minority, his essay serves as a warning on the instrumentalization of art as ideological propaganda.

Bojana Piškur considers the history of the NON-ALIGNED MOVEMENT, particularly its ethos of strength in diversity as a mode of resistance against the monolithic hegemonies of communism and Western liberal capitalism. She reflects on the movement, which, through solidarity and mutual respect, sought modes for self-determination in its respective societies and cultural practices, as well as the desire to open spaces for independent artistic thought and activity.

The Canadian activist and social scientist Max Haiven demonstrates the value of ambiguous artistic strategies that refuse the segregation of the cultural, political, and economic spheres. He interprets the work of indigenous artist Rebecca Belmore as a monstrous ghost that continues to haunt the Canadian settlers. It's a radical refusal of inclusion in their monocultural multiculturalism.

The Brazilian professor of art and politics of the body, Christine Greiner, analyzes the phenomenon of 'cultural cannibalism' as an artistic strategy to destabilize otherness or alterity. Cannibalism or 'anthropophagy' was utilized as a metaphor and a way of thinking about 'cultural strategies of devouring, that characterize the eclectic appetite and mestizo ways of producing life and arts in Brazil', according to Greiner.

Mi You considers the notion of Eurasia, tracing various forms of premodern global networks—trade, informational, mythical—and their implications for understanding monoculturalism today. Alongside examples from modern and contemporary art, Mi You focuses on ways of creating critical lenses and operational models from the past to insert into contemporary society. Central to her project of renewing Eurasia is the quest for a relational network encompassing nature as much as societies. She considers how such an ecology of practices can manifest in artistic, speculative and social practices.

Writer and curator Tirdad Zolghadr discusses ideas from his book *Traction* (2016) in a conversation with Nav Haq. Zolghadr considers the modes of 'indeterminancy' in contemporary artistic and curatorial work, in which he feels there is a constant deferral or diffusal of a statement, and thus from situating oneself, which ultimately serves to undermine the potential of art. Haq and Zolghadr compare 'indeterminacy' and 'ambiguity', looking to understand where the problems and potentials lie in art.

The Belgium-based visual anthropologist Paolo S.H. Favero explores the ambiguity of shadows which 'just as love' have an 'immense capacity to accumulate and overlap'. By reflecting on the design and architecture of Sufi mausolea in South Delhi (India) Favero states that shadow highlights the role of light and that it has a much more positive role in Eastern culture than it has in the Global North. Maybe it is worth rethinking darkness as a candle, which, as for the Persian poet Rumi, is 'the essence of making humans appreciate the true meaning of light, visions and knowledge', says Favero.

We also include artistic contributions from Hedwig Houben, Iman Issa and Public Movement, as practitioners exploring, in various ways, strategies and aesthetics of ambiguity. Hedwig Houben's work, typically in sculpture, performance, video, and text, considers the ambiguity of individual subjectivity, the personalities of people and objects, and the relations between them. Iman Issa's practice seeks to distinguish experiences of the personal from the collective. Working with a mode of aesthetics that deliberately creates a certain representational threshold, her works function through taking stories out of the specificity of a context, and opening them up to the associative potential of the viewer. Public Movement work primarily in performance, appropriating the rhetoric and aesthetics of state power in order to hold up a mirror to its modes of constructing a self-image.

We would like to thank all the contributors for their essential role in the making of this book. They have brought diverse and meaningful reflections on the notion of ambiguity. The publishing of *The Aesthetics of Ambiguity: Understanding and Addressing Monoculture* coincides with the exhibition *Monoculture: A Recent History* that takes place at M HKA (Museum of Contemporary Art Antwerp) during the autumn of 2020. Book and exhibition were preceded by the conference *Considering Monoculture*, co-convened by M HKA, Van Abbemuseum and deBuren, which took place in Brussels on 27–28 February 2020. Together they are to be considered as attempts to get to the heart of monoculturality, and its relations with ambiguity.

This book, conference, and exhibition are part of 'Our Many Europes', a four-year programme of the European museum confederation L'Internationale. The confederation brings together seven major European art institutions: MG+MSUM (Ljubljana, Slovenia); Museo Reina Sofía (Madrid, Spain); MACBA (Barcelona, Spain); M HKA (Antwerp, Belgium); Museum of Modern Art (Warsaw, Poland), SALT (Istanbul and Ankara, Turkey) and Van Abbemuseum (Eindhoven, the Netherlands); together with partners: HDK-Valand (Gothenburg, Sweden) and NCAD (Dublin, Ireland). We thank the Creative Europe programme for their support.

The Aesthetics of Ambiguity is the result of an ongoing collaboration between M HKA and the Antwerp Research Institute for the Arts (ARIA) at Antwerp University. Both partners are deeply interested in the quest for (more) ambiguity in order to avoid rigid borders or black-and-white polarity between cultures, as well as between art and scientific thinking. We want to promote ambiguity as a productive force to understand ourselves, how we relate to things and to each other, and to constitute new ways of thinking about art, society and cohabitation on this fabulous yet complicated place called 'Earth'.

References

— Bourdieu, Pierre. 1984. *Distinction: A Social Critique of the Judgement of Taste*. Cambridge, MA: Harvard University Press.
— Frenkel-Brunswik, Else. 1949. 'Intolerance of Ambiguity as an Emotional and Perceptual Personality Variable'. *Journal of Personality* 18 (1), pp. 108–143.
— Sartre, Jean-Paul. 1976. *Black Orpheus*, trans. S.W. Allen. Paris: Présence Africaine. First published in L.S. Senghor, ed., *Anthologie de la nouvelle poésie nègre et malgache de langue française, précédée de Orphée Noir par Jean-Paul Sartre*. Paris: Presses universitaires de France, 1948. 'ce racisme antiraciste est le seul chemin qui puisse mener à l'abolition des différences de race'.

The Rising Empire of Ambiguity
On the Art of Getting Beyond Identity Politics

Pascal Gielen

Let us try to assume our fundamental ambiguity.
Simone de Beauvoir, 1947

The irony of the logic of identity is that by seeking to reduce differently similar to the same, it turns the merely different into the absolutely other.
Irin Marion Young, 1999

Monsters

The power of identity politics, whether coming from feminist, ethnical, or nationalistic quarters, is that it generates energy for civil fight and political action. Those who feel that their individuality is not recognized, or not even acknowledged, tend to feel an urge towards articulation and identification. Slogans such as 'Black Lives Matter', 'My Body, My Choice', but also 'Leuven Flemish' result from a quest to find means and especially meanings to signify oneself. Culture and only culture provides the 'repertoire' of signs to set such a signifying process in motion (Gielen 2015). However, this process is always preceded by as yet undefined and therefore still unclear feelings of discontent, aversion, or sometimes even depression. Suppression and also collective repression do after all hinder subordinates in focusing their emotions. The transformation of hard to interpret affects, of feelings whose origin we find difficult to trace, but also of focused passions such as the wish for clear articulation may sometimes be in line with what Karl Marx has called the transition of 'Klasse an sich' to 'Klasse für sich'. And although the theory of social classes is often used to point out the problematic side of identity politics, the latter does take its cue from a similar mechanism. After all, doesn't class consciousness arise precisely by articulating an identity, however international this identity may be? The 'Klasse an sich' can only free itself from its unpleasant situation by first identifying and expressing itself (Marx 1974 [1867]). Like articulation and identification, expression is an essential step in any stage of emancipation.

The societal debate of the last century is hard to imagine without the problematics of identity and identification. How such identity logics exactly work has been the study object of many of the humanities, from philosophy, semiotics, psychoanalysis, anthropology, and sociology to cultural studies. Those studies have resulted in at least two helpful notions, specifically Jacques Derrida's 'differance' (1967) and Paul Vandenbroeck's 'negative

self-definition' (1987). As is common knowledge among philosophers, Derrida's homophonic 'differance' in French means
both 'delay' and 'difference'. The meaning of a word only arises
in delay, in which a particular word can only come after another
word, *and* distinct from previous or future words. Meaning,
in other words, only arises relationally and is therefore a matter
of convention, not of essence or substance. More broadly: it is
not a natural but a cultural thing. In short, the relation between
signifier and signified is arbitrary. These are by now well-known
but also somewhat worn-out insights from semiotics. Still, understanding the formal play between signifier, signified, and meaning
remains quite valuable in understanding the mechanisms of identity politics. For example, in *Gender Trouble* Judith Butler based
her constructivist theory about the difference between women
and men on it (Butler 1990). The biological difference in gender
pales compared to the distinction between, for example, feminine
and masculine traits, or matriarchal and patriarchal structures.
Or, a man can also act feminine and a woman can also run a
patriarchal organization—you know, as Margaret Thatcher did.
Identity is indeed not a matter of nature, but of culture. This also
means that it is always relative, as identity can only exist because
it has a relationship with other identities.

 With an analysis of the paintings of Hieronymus Bosch,
Pieter Bruegel the Elder, and others, in the mid-1980s Paul
Vandenbroek added another important insight: meaning is not
only constructed in the formal difference from another meaning.
Especially in identity forming, making a distinction usually happens in a negative and normative manner, hence Vandenbroeck's
'negative self-definition' (1987). What happens is that one defines
one's own identity by ascribing negative attributes to others in
order to then create a positive mirror image of oneself. In other words, the construction of identity does not exclusively arise
from a distinction between us and the other, but also from that
between a better 'we' versus a worse or inferior 'they'. At least
one's own values and norms are seen as better or 'more fitting'
for oneself then those of the other. The multicultural discourse
partly relies on the latter reasoning: everyone is entitled to their
own values, norms, and lifestyle, as long I may cherish mine or we
ours, or as long as ours are not threatened. However, no matter
how negative or different the others are painted in order to both
distance and confirm our own identity, the reference to the other

always remains anchored in our own identity. Just like 'we' need 'them', the word 'wo-man' needs the stem 'man'. Or, as psycho-analyst Julia Kristeva (1991) puts it: the other is always already inside ourselves, we are our own stranger. The thing that we don't want to be is, paradoxically, always already part of ourselves, no matter how hard we try to repress it. Taking this thought to its logical conclusion, it means, for example, that in every woman there is also a man, that Christianity also includes Islam, that de-mocracy cannot exist without an undemocratic momentum, that the constitution needs a-legal legislators, that a socialist also—secretly or not—harbours liberal ideals, and of course the reverse of all this. As we know from Bruno Latour's Actor-Network Theory: we are not either-or beings but and-and monsters (Latour 1994). In short, ambiguity is the rule and, who knows, is even our true 'nature' and therefore a unique identity is nothing but cul-ture. Or, less prosaically: the world consists of monsters, and pure beings only exist in the domain of the imaginary; only in fiction and art do we meet pure form; only in mathematics can the pure formula survive. By contrast, the empirical world is full of static. Reality is always more complex, more paradoxical, and perhaps much 'dirtier', but certainly more ambiguous.

Why Relativism Doesn't Work in Politics

Today, all identity theories need this relativism to maintain their own intellectual credibility, just like Butler secured academic fem-inism again with a hefty dose of constructivism. Relativism safe-guards all identity claims against essentialism, substantialism, nat-uralism, and even fundamentalism. Still, things that are relatively easily construed in theory are often hard to achieve in everyday social life. 'It is difficult to articulate positive elements of group af-finity without essentializing them', feminist political scientist Iris Marion Young (2011) admits. Especially in politics there always comes a moment at which the distinction between us and them becomes essentialistic and true ambiguity needs to be repressed. According to Dan Webb (2017)—following Chantal Mouffe and Jodi Dean—this is even the essence of politics. Politics cannot ex-ist without exclusion, without what we wish and want for ourselves but not for 'them'. Nowadays, just about all integration policies are based on it, at least in the Global North. 'You can only enjoy our prosperity if you subscribe to our values and norms.' In short, 'you' must become 'us', which in fact makes integration a synonym for assimilation. It should come as no surprise then that nowadays liberal philosophers like Francis Fukuyama speak of assimilation instead of integration, without blinking an eye. The others must subscribe to a country's national values and norms if they wish to make use of the social benefits provided by that state (Fukuyama 2019). If they do not comply, they will be permanently excluded. Apparently, politics needs that moment at which it can draw an essentialistic line between us and them, left and right, progressive and conservative. Politics draws strength from the momentum when the ranks are closed and all ambiguity is excluded. Webb:

> ... political decisions are always decisions of how *power* will be exerted, employed, or withheld. The moment of decision, a necessary prerequisite for political action, announces an antagonism, an 'us versus them', and a willingness to avow the symbolic violence (Webb 2017, p. 65).

So, concrete politics has little use for constructivist and other post-modern thought experiments. One can hardly perform a difficult balancing act between feminine and masculine traits when composing, say, an administrative body or political party's leadership in a responsible manner. Or, one may attempt to 'de-patriarchilize' an organization or decision-making processes, but such an enterprise would be rather absurd if the organization concerned is an exclusively male club. In other words, everyday identity politics always resorts to substantial and sometimes of course also natural distinctions in order to draw a straight line. How else is one supposed to enforce a quota of fifty per cent women? In the fight for equality the fact that we are already present in the other and, vice versa, this alterity is present in us, isn't really particularly helpful. It is a too soft or ethical argument that simply doesn't work in politics. Again, politics needs a moment of concretization, 'substantialization', or at least essentialization. This is also true of purely cultural constructs such as language, cultural diversity, or national identity. In order to make decisions, to make laws and to take measures politics must always cut the knot. Who is an economic refugee and who a political one? Who is integrated and proficient enough in the language and who isn't? Who is living below the poverty line and who isn't? All distinctions are gradual and open to interpretation, but in the final political decision between who is and who isn't, a strict line is always drawn.

The Pivoting Moment for Identity Politics

If politics needs essentialistic claims, the same goes—perhaps even more so—for identity politics. No matter how much feminist, postcolonial, or subaltern studies underline the relativity of identity constructs these days, both the activist and the politician will eventually have to resort to supposedly essential characteristics to guarantee a level playing field later. Striving for balance and equality is simply impossible without defining the unequals and therefore also not without pointing out a substantial difference (in treatment, colour, gender). And even though progressive academics know only too well that this attribution is also a matter of interpretation, the floating signifier will always have to arrive at a solidified meaning in order to perform a political act. This inevitable process of solidification does mean, however, that all emancipatory struggles always risk causing a conservative reflex. The emancipation of one section of the population can always turn into 'our-own-people-first' rhetoric; antiracism can turn into racist antiracism (Sartre 1976 [1949]); community forming into gated communities; feminism into gynocentrism; belief into fundamentalism; and love into obsession. The line between such binaries can be very thin and one can always discern historical pivoting moments at which the emancipation fighters start to behave in exactly the same manner as the enemy they are fighting against. And such moments are particularly interesting: the phase in which critical analyses based on cultural and therefore relative characteristics turn into substantial and 'naturalized' claims. It is not so much the turn itself that is interesting but the moment just before it occurs. One hypothesis is that it is precisely at that undecided or entropic junction that we may find a different politics than the one that is based on identity.

Organic Crisis

Ambiguity comes to the fore when we discover the otherness within ourselves. We can no longer ignore it, but we also don't know—yet—how to handle it. In other words, we have not yet articulated, defined, or labelled the other. In the realm of politics this takes the form of a liminal period of what Antonio Gramsci (1992) has once called 'an organic crisis'. According to him, such a crisis presents itself when an existing—political—system is terminal and a new one cannot yet be born. It is an interregnum that creates a kind of administrative vacuum in which all kinds of ecological, economic, political, and social crises occur in rapid succession for which the old ideology increasingly fails to provide acceptable or credible solutions. However, a new political paradigm cannot deliver this either, because it is not yet ready for it and cannot be satisfactorily articulated yet. One of the reasons for this is that such an articulation is substantially hampered by the representatives of the old system. Or, as mentioned earlier, repression works against articulation. It is during such a period of organic crisis that an emancipatory struggle can easily turn into what Gramsci calls 'Caesarism' (Gramsci 1992, p. 276). The interbellum was such a period. But are we not finding ourselves in a similar juncture again today? Although still thumping the bible of the free market, neoliberalism is finding it increasingly difficult to provide answers to the ecological and social problems it is generating itself. At the same time, there is, for the time being, no articulation of a full and credible alternative, no matter how hard progressive forces or the political left are trying. Anyway, they have a hard time convincing the majority of the population. And this is the momentum at which characters such as Viktor Orbán, Recep Tayyip Erdogan, Jair Bolsonaro, or Donald Trump come to the fore. After not even a century, the engine of the liberal revolution is already misfiring and reactionary and authoritarian ideas are gaining ground again. The success of the aforementioned gentlemen can in any case be seen as a symptom of the truly uncertain and ambiguous phase we find ourselves in. The fact that some politicians are frenetically trying to board things up is perhaps the best proof that we are in fact in a state of entropy. Everybody knows that urgent decisions have to be taken; everybody knows we should be heading in a different direction and yet we remain stuck in a situation of indecisiveness and half measures.

It is typically in times of organic crisis when Caesarism pushes forward that other political possibilities are repressed. While polarization is growing and the gap between ideological sides is becoming wider and wider, the chance for real radical alternatives, paradoxically, evaporates. The opposing parties entrench themselves by, among other things, centralizing their own identity, as mentioned before. Sweet multiculturalism disintegrates into bitterly fighting monocultures because just like monoculturalism, multiculturalism was not satisfied with ambiguity. Traditionally, periods of organic crisis are not the best electoral times for give-and-take parties in the political centre. Everyone is looking for a way out within their own idea of what is right, and doxas and dogmas are accentuated on both sides. Typical of such periods, however, is that below the radar a growing liminal realm of unimaginable arenas, of unseen possibilities, and even of both ideologically and legally prohibited practices unfolds. This is a zone where the trusted compass between right and left, between conservative and progressive, between localism and globalism goes haywire because these political vectors are no longer functioning, to quote Bruno Latour (Latour 2018). This notwithstanding, it is on this grey, also a-legal terrain that ambiguous politics find fertile soil and truly new constitutions are being prepared. It is perhaps no coincidence that this is also the terrain where various social positions meet and where the distinction between professions becomes less sharp. Both laymen and experts as well as grassroots movements and established institutions find themselves in the same situation there, as the terrain is unknown to all of them and their futures are equally uncertain. This is where artists become politicians, judges start operating as activists, politicians as relief workers, doctors as resistance fighters, and 'objective' scientists as moral opinion leaders. As things above ground become increasingly rigid, underground heterogeneity and liquidity are on the rise. This also means that identities, including professional identities, transmute or even remain totally open sometimes. In other words, what appeared to be irreconcilable ideas and practices fuse together into the most natural conglomerate rates during Gramsci's periods of 'organic crisis'. What look like nothing but paradoxes and contradictions above ground, accumulates underground until the moment that this expanding mass has no alternative but to break through the floor.

Aesthetical Ambiguity

It is hardly surprising that during such periods artists often come forward. They are after all very talented and often very well-trained in both creating and handling ambiguity. They do so, for example, by designing a visual language or a form of word art that is open to multiple interpretations. Isn't that exactly where the difference between prose and poetry lies, especially in that zone where meanings and signifiers become floating. Artists with a too unambiguous or too evident message are in any case often criticized and accused of making 'bad' art or simply 'not art' at all. Being 'unambiguous', being 'preacher-ish' are still powerful invectives in art criticism. Perhaps this is why many artists prefer not to explain their work, preferring to leave its meaning 'open'. To an extent, ambiguity stands for quality in the contemporary professional art world. How different art is from politics in that regard. In politics, ambiguity tends to have a negative connotation. In political science the term 'ambiguity politics' refers primarily to the phenomenon of politicians not really speaking their mind in order to avoid electoral loss. Professional politicians often don't reveal their personal ideas or their preference for addressing certain social issues because they know that their views may not be very popular and may cost them votes.

Aesthetic ambiguity might be accused of using the same tactics. Allowing for multiple interpretation could, after all, appeal to a larger and more diverse audience of art lovers. However, as we know from cultural-sociological research, only a small portion of the population responds to an alchemy of meanings and identities (Bourdieu 1974). A large majority actually avoids heterogeneity and doesn't endure ambiguity for very long. This is rather regrettable because at the same time scientific studies point to a solid positive correlation—although not a causal one—between on the one hand being able to handle ambiguity and ambiguous visual language and, on the other hand, being open to the other (Frenkel-Brunswik 1949). For example, someone who knows how to deal with ambiguous codes and information is significantly less likely to build up a racist set of values than someone who doesn't. Those who know how to handle ambiguity also feel less need for coherence or understand better that the world around them and the times they live in are full of paradoxes and contradictions. In other words, they don't need to fully understand the world in order to live happily in it. It would be worthwhile to investigate whether ambiguity might be actively deployed in politics. To be absolutely clear: this does not refer to the abovementioned politicological views of not very sincere administrators, but to a politics that teaches people to actively deal with ambiguity, thereby deflating the myth of transparent identity. In order to understand what such politics might look like, it seems appropriate, for the above reasons, to take a look at the art world.

One Man Standing
On 17 June 2013 at 6 PM, Turkish performance artist Erdem Gündüz decides to stand still, all alone, for a month, at Istanbul's

Taksim Square and stare at the—meanwhile demolished—Atatürk Cultural Centre. From the façade of the centre hangs a banner with the likeness of Mustafa Kemal Atatürk, the man who once made Turkey a secular state. Gündüz begins his action on the same day that the Erdogan government prohibits protests following the heavy riots in Gezi Park. The performer thus stands not only literally before Atatürk, but also symbolically diametrically opposite the Caesarism personified by Erdogan in his homeland. Gündüz does not carry a banner, does not chant slogans, and neatly complies with the ban on assembling by acting alone. All this makes his action most ambiguous, both for those happening to pass by and for the police. Is this a protest, art, or a meaningless act of a disturbed individual? Should the police intervene? Would that be right or even lawful? In any case, it took a while before bystanders began to notice the performer and started to twitter about him, alerting the police that something was afoot. Around 2 AM they finally did intervene because supporters were assembling around Gündüz and only then the action of the Turkish performer was labelled a protest. It could only last as long as his identity remained fluid. Is he an artist, an activist, or just some lunatic? Only when the situation is identified, the action is terminated. Gündüz' act, whether or not political, artistic, or hopeless, does however teach us something about what may characterize a possible politics of ambiguity. The least we can learn from his performance is that such a politics must be playful, variable, urban, and even a tiny bit erotic.

It is obvious that Gündüz is performing. He does even more: he brings one of the by now well-known artistic tricks of conceptual dance outside the walls of the theatre, namely *standing still*. This play with the rules of art, this breaking with the convention that in a dance performance there should be dancing, is applied by Gündüz in public space. He is protesting without protesting. Or, rather, the performer ignores the known codes of activism, precisely in order to make his action a success. Just as the conceptual choreographer once managed to annoy a dance audience, Gündüz now does so with the passers-by in a square and certainly with the police, who have trouble identifying the matter. This playfulness is in sharp contrast with the gravity of activists who gradually entrench themselves in their own cause, their own right, their own identity. Gündüz too is fighting with indignation against the political situation but he doesn't posit his own 'right' against it. For instance, during his action the performer refuses to speak or identify himself. Afterwards, he tells the BBC: 'I'm just one protester, I'm just one artist... I'm nothing.' Gündüz opposes, clearly identifies a hostile 'they' but without flying his own political colours. Thanks to this playfulness he remains ambiguous and avoids ending up in bitterly vindictive rhetoric or dogmatism. That same playfulness also makes sure that his identity remains variable and this variability in turn guarantees that the play can continue to be played. Precisely because Gündüz refuses to play a single role or choose a single identity he remains fluid. He is not either an artist *or* an activist *or* a lunatic, but an artist *and* an activist *and* a lunatic *and*... nothing. This 'monstrous' aspect is what lends his action a certain erotic appeal. That what is left unsaid, what is indistinct, arouses curiosity. Whereas identity politics frequently repulses people by continuously harping on something, ambiguity politics seduces them by creating confusion. It anticipates the pleasure and excitement of being drawn from the safety of your routines, of being confronted with something that is unknown, incomprehensible, or surprising. Precisely because we do not know what to expect from ambiguity, we are tempted to flirt with it. Like someone parading the streets we want to know what's around the corner and then we want to know what's around the next corner. With the previously quoted Young we could indeed say that ambiguity politics is radically urban. The political scientist contrasts the city, in normative terms, with a community aspiring to a uniform identity, such as local communities or the nation state. An urban living environment, by contrast, does not consist of equals, not of people who recognize each other, but of a 'being together of strangers' (Young 2011, p. 237).

> City dwellers are together, bound to one another, in what should be and sometimes is a single polity. Their being together entails some common problems and common interests, but they do not create a community of shared final ends, of mutual identification and reciprocity (Young 2011, p. 238).

One cannot base a hyper-diverse and mobile city on a preconceived blueprint, nor can one base a policy on it. Ambiguity politics, by contrast, is satisfied with the fact that the world is full of loose ends. Unlike a canal with straight banks, this attitude provides a meandering river of possibilities. In a small-scale and modest way, Gündüz' action demonstrates how to break open this social horizon of multiple use and differentiation and keep it open. This always carries the risk of being ostracized and of losing one's own identity. Gündüz risks being rejected by the professional art world because his work may be labelled as pure activist or political from now on. At the same time, it is possible that activists and politicians do not accept him either because his action is not explicit enough, is too artistic, indeed too ambiguous. In other words, the performer risks falling in between known and predefined identities. Still, it seems necessary to experiment with such ambiguous practices, as perhaps they contain a key for addressing issues of monoculturalism and neonationalism, multiculturalism and identity politics. After all, out of the contradictions and segregations raised by such political formations rises an unstoppable 'in-between' category. This ambiguous population category is not meaningless like an empty signifier, but is on the contrary full of meaning as it is overpopulated with all those falling between the monocultures of the multicultural world. Precisely this subset, this overlap and fusion between different identities and cultures will define the future. Precisely this 'in-between' area is the compost for a mixture that will grow to become the new majority of the world population. This irreversibly growing reality will inevitably classify all forms of identity, monoculture, and multi-culture as superstitions that were once Enlightened. Or, to put it somewhat paradoxically: here lies the constitution for a new monoculture, but this time it will be a hyper-heterogenous empire of ramshackle causalities. This is the realm of ambiguity, a geopolitical space the *geos* of which—to quote Latour (2018) once more—does not refer to a bordered-off terrain but to the entire Earth.

References

— Beauvoir, Simone de. 1947 (1976). *The Ethics of Ambiguity*. New York: Open Road.
— Bourdieu, Pierre. 1974. 'Les fractions de la classe dominante et les modes d'appropriation des oeuvres d'art'. *Information sur les sciences sociales* 13, no. 3, pp. 7-32.
— Butler, Judith. 1990. *Gender Trouble: Feminism and the Subversion of Identity*. New York and London: Routledge.
— Derrida, Jacques. 1967. *L'Ecriture et la différence*. Paris: Seuil.
— Frenkel-Brunswik, Else. 1949. 'Intolerance of Ambiguity as an Emotional and Perceptual Variable'. *Journal of Personality* 18, pp. 108-143.
— Fukuyama, Francis. 2019. *Identity: Contemporary Identity Politics and the Struggle for Recognition*. London: Profile Books.
— Gielen, Pascal, ed. 2015. *No Culture, No Europe: On the Foundation of Politics*. Amsterdam: Valiz.
— Gramsci, Antonio. 1992. *Prison Notes*. New York: Columbia University Press.
— Kristeva, Julia. 1991. *De vreemdeling in onszelf*. Amsterdam: Atlas Contact.
— Latour, Bruno. 1994. *Wij zijn nooit modern geweest*. Amsterdam: Van Gennep.
—. 2017. *Waar kunnen we landen? Politieke oriëntatie in het Nieuwe Klimaatregime*. Amsterdam: Octavo.
— Marx, Karl. 1974 (1867). *Capital: A Critique of Political Economy. Volume 1*. New York: Vintage Books.
— Sartre, Jean-Paul. 1976. *Black Orpheus*. Paris: Présence Africaine.
— Vandenbroeck, Paul. 1987. *Beeld van de andere, vertoog over het zelf: Over wilden en narren, boeren en bedelaars*. Antwerp: Koninklijk Museum voor Schone Kunsten.
— Webb, Dan. 2017. *Critical Urban Theory, Common Property, and 'the Political': Desire and Drive in the City*. New York and London: Routledge.
— Young, Iris Marion. 2011. *Justice and the Politics of Difference*. Princeton and Oxford: Princeton University Press.

Ambiguity and Liberalisms

Artistic and Institutional Practices as a Sphere of Cultural Influence

Nav Haq

The resulting syndrome I have proposed to call 'intolerance of ambiguity.' A rigid cognitive superstructure in which everything opaque and complex is avoided as much as possible is super-imposed upon the conflict-ridden emotional understructure. In effect, this merely duplicates slavery to authority rather than remedying it. Now there is not only slavery to the authority of the other person; there is also slavery to the authority of the stimulus. In other words, the attitude towards a perceptual stimulus or a cognitive task mirrors the attitude towards authority.[1]

The subtle but profound distortion of reality in the course of the elimination of ambiguities is in the last analysis precipitated by the fact that stereotypical categorizations can never do justice to all the possible aspects of reality. So long as a culture provides socially accepted outlets for suppressed impulses, smooth functioning and fair adjustment can be achieved within the given framework.[2]

Else Frenkel-Brunswik

We start from the relative failure of identity politics. The historical movement of identity politics generally associated with the 1980s in regions of the Western World, together with its recent, more internationalized resurgence in the socially-liberal mainstream, could be considered as a variety of institutional critique, with its motivations to address power, but also with its pitfalls and recuperations. The desire to create social awareness and provide space, voice, and opportunities to those groups subjected to processes of minoritization has on the one hand pushed for wider participation and recognition. Yet identity politics has come to be considered as dogmatic, to the degree that the pushback has also been forceful, even providing legitimacy and traction for far-right populists. Its emphasis on assertion does not always lead to lasting influence, and is often seen by its most vociferous opponents as ideological bursts of liberal groupthink or even as a kind of false consciousness. In the artistic sphere, identity politics has led to a push for equality of representation. But along with it, have come representational borders, demanding that cultural differences never be encroached, misplaced, or even challenged.[3] With such emphasis on constituencies of biography and their exclusive relation to artistic content, it is easy to see it as having led to a pluralization of identity monocultures. We might even refer to this as the 'Balkanization of representation'. It is the illiberal side of identity liberalism, hardening its intolerance even of other liberalisms. Identity politics finds itself in a quandary of politically correct lexicology, administered relativism, and the policing of creative parameters. Such unambiguous politics of identity, almost Warholian in its formal and verbal characteristics of surface representation and replication, offers little oxygen to the rights and necessities to explore otherness and broaden our subjectivity. In the worst cases, identity politics adopts the rigid stimulus-response relations of propaganda, projecting myths of authenticity. It should be obvious that people are more than their representation, and that representation is also *only* representation, and not in itself the same as equality.

Tolerance or intolerance of perceived differences, whether in terms of the established identity constituencies of race, ethnicity, gender, and sexuality, but also differences in ideological partiality, religion, or socio-economic conditions and even creative outlook, need to find new spaces of negotiation. The scales of tolerance and intolerance in society always exist, being characteristic of the human psyche, and can fluctuate depending on the direction societies and their communities move in. However, there are moments when societies are influenced by competing ideological forces to the point of polarization, resulting in the collective hardening of tolerances and intolerances. Such crystallization of mass psychology, where a culture seeking to identify levels of conformity to one's communitarian self-image—leading to such homogenous expression of intolerance—can be identified as an intolerant form of monoculture. Perhaps the most recent manifestations of *Kulturkampf* or 'culture wars' in the late twentieth and early twenty-first centuries contest this spectrum of tolerance and intolerance. There are similarly many examples of when the artistic field can become a site of contention. Broadly seen as socially liberal, art is often accused of elitism, ideological superiority, and provocation. We know art finds itself negotiating issues of freedom of expression or censorship when it reaches borders of sensitivity, but this is also the case when it is not understood or appreciated. Art, along with its institutions, can find itself subject to the influence of ideologies from neo-liberalism to populism, even when not directly led by them. It becomes a space of vulnerability in these circumstances. Yet as the expression of the human creative capacity, its existence is as significant as ever. For this reason, art and its institutional practices must take it upon themselves to find new reasoning and meaning for their role in society. From the artistic field, how might we start to define and address monocultural intolerance? What new kind of liberalism do we want? And what kind of artistic and institutional practices can we equip ourselves with to form a positive sphere of influence on society?

Throughout the twentieth century we can identify several key thinkers who explored, in various ways, monoculture or cultural homogeneity. But perhaps some of the most relevant and thought-provoking among them are those who consider monoculture as it relates to the ambiguous. The work of pioneering psychoanalyst Else Frenkel-Brunswik is significant here, but we might also think of the ideas of philosophers Simone de Beauvoir[4] and Julia Kristeva[5]. In her attempt to understand ethnocentricity as a characteristic of the authoritarian mind, Frenkel-Brunswik developed ideas described as 'Ambiguity Tolerance-Intolerance'. First introduced in 1949, Ambiguity Tolerance-Intolerance is a psychological construct that measures the relationship individuals have with various ambiguous stimuli. In this personality-centred analysis, Frenkel-Brunswik makes a correlation between liberalisms of perception, cognition, and social outlook. In simple terms, intolerance of ambiguity may be defined as the tendency to interpret ambiguous situations as sources of threat. Whereas tolerance of ambiguity is the tendency to see ambiguous situations as desirable. 'Ambiguity' may for example be in terms of physical characteristics of another, such as a person of ambiguous race, ethnicity, gender, or sexuality, but it may also be in terms of ambiguous situations, images, or objects. In her study, which was primarily with children, she used this measure to test the hypothesis that children who are ethnically prejudiced also tend to reject ambiguity more so than their peers. Such individuals who tested as ambiguity-intolerant, were unable to genuinely understand the self and others effectively, instead seeking power and success and relying on rigid stereotypes to ensure order and safety.

There is science before, and there is science after. Like many renowned psychoanalysts, such as Sigmund Freud and Melanie Klein, Frenkel-Brunswik was from a Jewish family, who fled Austria to escape anti-Jewish persecution. We know of the race science, or 'racial hygiene' that informed Nazi ideology—the dark, eugenicist side of science, that sought to form an unambiguous image of cultural homogeneity, as a system to cleanse society of everyone else. In her research, Frenkel-Brunswik refers to psychologist Erich Rudolph Jaensch, permanent president of the German Psychological Association under the Third Reich, who developed an influential body of policies outlining Nazism as a biological movement. As well as outlining ideas of racial purity, along with considering blood mixture an 'abnormal state of affairs', Jaensch also describes the anti-German and German ways of looking. The 'antitype' to the German had inclinations towards the aesthetical, intellectual, and playful; whereas German perception would possess rigid, or unambiguous, stimulus-response relationships. Thus we see how Nazi pseudoscience saw the biological in relation to perception, and thus monoculturalism also as a mode of seeing. Frenkel-Brunswik settled in America, developing her earlier work in personality studies, and collaborating with contemporaries such as Theodor Adorno and Daniel Levinson.[7] Psychoanalysis may be seen as something that survived the Holocaust. Thus, it comes as no surprise it is a discipline that has sought to understand the human mind, including its extremes.

It is a great shame that Frenkel-Brunswik is not as widely known as some of her contemporaries, as her research offers valuable analyses for social and visual culture. The primary characteristics that describe intolerance of ambiguity, according to Frenkel-Brunswik's analysis, are as follows: the need for categorization and for certainty; an inability to allow good and bad traits to exist in the same person; acceptance of statements representing a black-white view of life; a preference for the familiar over the unfamiliar; a rejection of the unusual or different; resistance to fluctuating stimuli; early selection and dedication to one solution in an ambiguous situation; and premature resolution. The intolerant also have a tendency to be authoritarian, dogmatic, closed-minded, ethnically prejudiced, uncreative, anxious and aggressive, along with other characteristics perceived negatively that we can associate with the intolerant kind of monoculture. In contrast, characteristics of tolerance of ambiguity include: the embrace of multi-dimensionality and complexity, differentiation and creativity. Crucially, the tolerant also harbour less prejudice. However, it is important that Tolerance-Intolerance is seen as variable on a spectrum. We should also note that, although her research assumes that there is a correlation between dealing with ambiguity in perception, cognition, and encounters in everyday life—in other words, those who are open to the ambiguous or paradoxical stimuli being also more open to the Other, their own subjectivity and in society—it did not extend far into whether there is causality. But with its basis in perception, it offers an empirical basis for the artistic field to work with.

Research shows us that being too far on either end of the spectrum of ambiguity tolerance–intolerance can be detrimental to mental health. Frenkel-Brunswik stated: 'To be sure, in psychoanalysis is discovered primarily the field of emotion, through the phenomenon of ambivalence. Conscious love of extreme and exaggerated intensity is viewed with the same suspicion by the psychoanalyst as are extreme feelings of hate.'[8] This might even suggest something to us about the extreme love and extreme hate of minorities as they manifest in the typical dichotomy of liberal-left and conservative-right ideologies. Ultimately though, a monocultural society does not necessarily have to be prejudiced. Cultural homogeneity does not strictly imply ethnocentricity, one-dimensionality, or impoverishment either. A monoculture's self-image can also be born from an emancipatory imperative, such as in the context of anti-colonial movements—we might see *Négritude* in Senegal as one key case study here—or communities impoverished under the negative neo-colonial effects of globalization. They can still be transformational or inclusive. But the characteristics of ambiguity intolerance can also be seen as representing those of the intolerant kind of monoculture: the kind of monoculture at risk of becoming ideological, and that is unwilling even to acknowledge let alone accept the presence of the natural 'multiculture' of individual subjectivities. We hear such words as 'populism', 'ethnic nationalism' or 'identitarianism' to describe such movements. But just as with the understanding of other cultural groups that are subject to prejudice and stereotyping, it is important that we do not look at the intolerant monoculture in terms of an essentialism. In fact, we might identify an institutional role for exploring this otherness.

Frenkel-Brunswick's analysis of the correlation between perception, cognition, and social outlook in the understanding of personality also, significantly, included experiments in perceptual ambiguity, and visual stimuli. However, being confined to simple scientific motifs—for example Brunswick refers to an image of a cat, a dog, and then images of something in between a cat and a dog to represent the ambiguous—the tests had limited aesthetic range. For this reason, it can be meaningful to attempt to position her theories in relation to the experience of visual art and to art history. One of the most striking historical demonstrations of ideological monoculture in the cultural field was through the infamous 1937 *Entartete Kunst* (Degenerate Art) exhibition staged in Nazi Germany. We can read this as an example of ambiguity intolerance in extremis, holding up the modernist avant-garde as an aberration. Avant-garde art was an aesthetic pollutant, Jews and other minorities were a racial pollutant, therefore to be eradicated. Nazism sought instead a decidedly unambiguous ethno-centric conception of culture inspired by Greco-Roman civilization. Appropriating and racializing such historical imaginary, along with eugenics and *Freikörperkultur* alike, was part of the course of defining the Aryan race. We see this reflected, for example, in the art exhibited in the editions of the *Große Deutsche Kunstausstellung* (Great German Art Exhibition) that took place eight times in Munich between 1937 and 1944. Nazi art can be seen as an example of how art looks under extreme monocultural ideology, when taken to its logical conclusion. Both *Entartete Kunst* and *Große Deutsche Kunstausstellung* were exhibitions as propaganda, displaying environmentally controlled correlations of art, culture, race, and pseudoscience.

The notion of ambiguity also provides us with a new lens for considering the work of artist Joseph Beuys in the period of the post-war avant-garde. It is well known that Beuys served in the Luftwaffe during the Second World War, and sustained several injuries. The experience of war was a central influence on his practice in the period of the rebuilding of Germany. Beuys' work embraced aesthetic ambiguity, with material qualities that utilized such things as fat, felt, honey, blood, live animals (the coyote), and dead animals (the hare). The aesthetic ambiguity of his work might even be seen as a kind of 'denazification' of art necessary in Germany in the post-war period. Along with its aesthetics, his practice was intended to be more broadly emancipatory, bringing together intellectual discourse, actions, education, politics, and activism, seeking to broaden the potential of art and knowledge, and perspectives on culture, nature, and society. These different facets of Beuys' work together sought to influence the tolerance of ambiguity, via its liberalisms of perception (via aesthetics), cognition (via its discursive qualities), and social outlook (via its societal propositions). We can see Beuys as a propaganda machine, producing many statements, manifestos and forums seeking to influence close followers and the broader public alike. Ironically, it must be said, Beuys was curiously authoritarian as a teacher or shaman figure, who also had potent mass-media sensibility. But to a high degree it was effective, by introducing aesthetics that stood in stark contrast to both Nazi art and Western modernist art, and also by adding a social and convivial dimension to art, climate activism, and appreciation of cultural and political diversity.

When Beuys would talk about 'Der Dritte Weg' (The Third Way), or asking to 'Show your wound', he was seeking action for finding new dimensions and possibilities, and creative reconciliations in response to the ideological status quo. The Third Way was intended as an emancipatory mode of existence between the levels of the individual and the societal, encouraging people to discover their individual energy and potential, whilst at the same time being committed to their responsibility towards society. The 'wound', as Beuys described it, was a violent chasm that had been made between the 'rationality' of the West, and the 'intuition' of the East, that he felt had led to impoverishment, enslavement, and catastrophe. In Beuys' eyes, a reconciliation between the two modes should be found. Such ideas also manifested in Beuys' interest in Eurasia—an understanding of the continental landmass as a plurality of cultures that stood in opposition to the modernistic constructs of nation state and national boundaries. These ideas would manifest in experimental art, actions, and propaganda. Such propositions sought a multi-dimensional approach to life and the world, as a free-flowing transformational process. It is a call to tolerate and even embrace ambiguity. Beuys was often accused of being vague or non-concrete in his pronouncements, and there is clear justification for this, but the sentiment of a multi-faceted worldview is clear and his ideas have had a significant and lasting influence. We can see his roles in the German Green Party (Die Grünen) and the Free International University movement as two palpable, enduring examples of this.

The ambiguity of art has been a staple of theoretical discourse for several decades, and we might understand this ambiguity on several levels, from the ontological to the aesthetic. In terms of the ontological status of art, however we decide to look at what it is, art proves time and again to be baffling. The complex tangle of emotions and conundrums around the philosophical question *is it art?* always concludes that it really is its own category of experience.[9] Just like its makers, contemporary art has its dialectical capabilities—simultaneously possessing different characteristics and statuses in any one moment. It can be utopian whilst negative, or shocking whilst banal. It can be both with and without relations to its creator or its cultural specificity. There are no limits to the feelings it can evoke. On the aesthetic plane, art can be 'good' whilst 'bad', open to judgments and readings on a vast scale of nuance. It can be both abstract—as in a non-figurative form of representation—and concrete. It can be simultaneously text and image. And ever since 'non-art' expanded the definition of art, it can be made of anything. Art is fundamentally ambiguous, and its ambiguity offers a negotiation of sorts. It prises open the rigid stimulus-response relationship, inviting us to experience and interpret these different characteristics and dimensions in their simultaneity. The question is: is one willing or fearful to undertake the challenge of exploring one's liberalisms? And if one is fearful, then it raises the subsequent question of how this negotiation might be mediated.

There can be an emancipatory potential to ambiguity. The avant-garde of the twentieth century, exemplified by the very public figure of Beuys, but also by many practitioners over the last century until the present moment, has brought a paradigm shift in visual culture. We can think of the androgyny and surreal ethnography of Hannah Höch's collages, of the corporeal exuberance of Carol Rama's images, the para-linguistics of Marcel Broodthaers' poetic oeuvre, the fleshy existentialism of Paul Thek's sculptures, or the intersectional abstraction of Haegue Yang's installations. A lot of the best art is simply uncategorizable. The influence that art can have, particularly through its presence in the public sphere, does not always have to be immediate, and it is perhaps best when slow-burning. When they emerged, early modernist, abstract, non-representational, and conceptual artworks were derided, whether as degenerate in extreme situations, but even in cultural metropoles considered to be 'progressive' as vulgar or immoral. Yet the public perception, acceptance, and positive sentiment has developed over time, expanding what is culturally acceptable. Contemporary art is a constant presence of ambiguity in society and has been for a long time, particularly in the West, and much of it is challenging, horizon-broadening and informative. In contrast to the artistic movement of identity politics, there are also many artists who challenge the conventionally assumed connection between identity and identification. Beyond generic visibility politics and its formal modes of representation, many artists are dealing, through various means and modes, with individual subjectivity in terms of complexity and the ambiguous.[10] Ambiguity and ambiguous positionality can be strategies of existence, resistance, and freedom. It can be emancipatory for practitioners to explore life and relations to the world in this way, and can have influence on those that experience it.

The rapid proliferation of art institutions in the twentieth and early twenty-first centuries, could be seen as a marker of broadening social liberalism. From the modernist avant-garde to contemporary post-media practices and everything in between, local and international, art has become largely mainstream and even popular. Perhaps though, the work of institutions in presenting art and artistic developments, when seen as a sphere of influence, also takes long and sometimes barely perceptible lengths of time. The ambiguity tolerance has been built over decades. Institutional practices in themselves could be seen as influencers of personality, working at the intersecting liberalisms of perception, cognition, and social outlook. They also, in this sense, facilitate the meeting point of visual culture, development of new ideas, and diverse audiences. Operating as a separate channel to the media, but sometimes in conjunction with them, institutional practice can open doors of negotiation, perception, and freedom of thought. For this reason, it is culturally important that they remain spaces for ambiguity in defiance of ideological confinement. In this era, when cultural institutions, particularly those within the public sphere, are seeking to identify what and who they are for, and what values they possess, we can propose a new philosophical answer. The philosophical dimension of museums and cultural institutions, and their place in society, is—*to increase tolerance of ambiguous things.*

Rather than resigning ourselves to homogeneous artistic expression under (impending) ideological monoculture, we may ask: *What could become the role and modality of the arts within the context of increasing monoculture?* Whilst galleries and museums have a good understanding of the perceptual and cognitive liberalisms, the social one can often be unresolved or disconnected. This is often confined to the generalized 'footfall' of art lovers and the curious coming through the doors, as well as engagement with children. While this is commendable, new relations to their publics are worth investing in, and are perhaps even essential in order to determine a future role and vitality. Museums and galleries have, gradually and partially, moved away from purely telling audiences how to look at or read artworks, towards privileging subjectivity and interpretation.[11] In this sense, just like the art they house, they are against the homogenizing effects of the rigid stimuli-response relationship. And these have been important steps towards creating new conditions for both audience and artwork. The ambiguity of art, the category of experience that it is, functions as a conduit to discover and affirm one's undiscovered liberalisms. Institutions, however, are greatly hindering their societal potential by catering primarily for the already-converted—the ambiguity-tolerant. If they are to truly fulfil their role of increasing tolerance of ambiguity, then they must look beyond.

As civil society institutions, galleries and museums ought to provide opportunities of engagement for the different constituencies that make up contemporary society. Institutions are secularized, not only transcendentally, but within the gamut of the Western political they provide, and so, at least in principle, are open towards the spectrum of ideological partialities. With long-term engagement, individuals, groups, and other constituent bodies could then participate in spaces of negotiation at the levels of the perceptual, cognitive, and the social. If organized on a qualitative level, such experiences can be taken away, and be in their own way emancipatory. Such a role, supporting 'agonistic' relations with and between constituencies, and with aesthetics and artistic work, can be unique and influential in the public sphere. And though institutions should be open, they should not be passive. As Pascal Gielen states: 'The journey from one world to another sometimes needs to be jumpstarted. In the recent past, institutions seemed almost embarrassed to take on a truly guiding role, to suggest designs for communality based on their own value frameworks. The fear of coming across as patronizing or pedantic has paralyzed their social performativity.'[12] With grounding in values they believe in, and on empirical foundations, museums and galleries can aim for a leading role as civil society institutions.

This philosophical dimension based on ambiguity can act as a revitalizing imperative for the sphere of art, including in the situation of ideological monoculture. Art, along with its institutionalization, sometimes finds itself in the position of negotiating to maintain the independence essential to its vitality. Justifications can sometimes be posed, rightly or wrongly, for different forms of cultural confinement or identitarianism—from ideological protectionism built on fear and prejudice to minoritarian protectionism based on visibility. But as impatient as we may be regarding social justice and equality, there will not typically be a quick-fix solution. Art institutions such as galleries and museums provide a space for the subjectivities and intelligence of artists and audiences alike, and can influence society. To revisit the quote that opens this essay, Frenkel-Brunswik stated: 'So long as a culture provides socially accepted outlets for supressed impulses, smooth functioning and fair adjustment can be achieved within the given framework.' The interlinked liberalisms of perception, cognition, and social outlook sit succinctly in relation to the arts and visual culture. But we must understand that when we deal with identities, we must do so with the knowledge that they incorporate ambiguity, and that our handling of identity should be dogma-free. This institutional responsibility should work to be patient, meaningful and emancipatory, with the conviction that aesthetic and experiential impoverishment is also ultimately societal impoverishment.

Notes

1. Else Frenkel-Brunswik, in sub-section: *Patterns of Perception and Thought; Intolerance and Ambiguity*, from the essay 'Environmental Controls and the Impoverishment of Thought', first published in *Totalitarianism*, ed. C.J. Friedrich (Cambridge, MA: Harvard University Press, 1954), pp. 171–202. Reprinted in *Psychological Issues* Volume VIII/Number 3, Monograph 32: 'Else Frenkel-Brunswik: Selected Papers', eds. Nanette Heiman and Joan Grant (New York: International Universities Press, 1974), p. 275.

2. Ibid., p. 276.

3. Though centred on the American context, Mark Lilla makes a convincing case on the failure of identity politics, arguing for a post-identity liberalism: 'Such people are not actually reacting against the reality of our diverse America (they tend, after all, to live in homogeneous areas of the country). But they are reacting against the omnipresent rhetoric of identity, which is what they mean by "political correctness". Liberals should bear in mind that the first identity movement in American politics was the Ku Klux Klan, which still exists. Those who play the identity game should be prepared to lose it.' Mark Lilla, 'The End of Identity Liberalism', *New York Times*, 20 November 2016.

4. De Beauvoir describes the emancipatory potential that can come from the understanding that as individuals we are not guided by ideology, nor by deity, and rather that we are fundamentally ambiguous. 'Let us try to assume our fundamental ambiguity. It is in the knowledge of the genuine conditions of our life that we must draw our strength to live and our reason for acting.' In Simone de Beauvoir, *The Ethics of Ambiguity*, trans. Bernard Frechtman (New York: Philosophical Library/Open Road, 2011 [1947]), p. 8.

5. Primarily in Julia Kristeva, *Powers of Horror: An Essay on Abjection* (New York: 1982 [1980]), in which she describes a modern condition of feeling horror in encounters, both mental and physical, when experiencing ambiguous encounters at the breakdown between self and other.

6. Erich Rudolph Jaensch, *Der Gegentypus: Psychologisch-anthropologische Grundlagen deutscher Kulturphilosophie, ausgehend von dem was wir überwinden wollen* (Leipzig: Barth, 1938); translated as *The Antitype: Psychological-Anthropological Foundations of German Cultural Philosophy Based on What We Must Overcome*.

7. Such as their work together with Else Frenkel-Brunswik and Nevitt Sanford on the book *The Authoritarian Personality* (New York: Harper & Brothers, 1950).

8. Frenkel-Brunswik, *Patterns of Perception and Thought*, p. 88.

9. I particularly enjoy the writings of Thierry de Duve on the question of what art is. See, for example his series of texts published in *Artforum* during 2013 and 2014. 'Pardon My French' (October 2013), 'Don't Shoot the Messenger' (November 2013), 'Why Was Modernism Born in France?' (January 2014), 'The Invention of Non-Art: A History' (February 2014), and 'The Invention of Non-Art: A Theory' (March 2014) and 'This is Art': Anatomy of a Sentence (April 2014).

10. The exhibition *Don't You Know Who I Am? Art After Identity Politics* presented at M HKA – Museum of Contemporary Art Antwerp in 2016 explored this 'post-identity' mode of practice in contemporary art. Information can be found at the exhibition's special microsite: http://afteridentity.muhka.be/.

11. Nicholas Serota provides a useful historical account of the gradual transitions of museum practices in their modes of display, in *Experience or Interpretation: The Dilemma of Museums of Modern Art* (London: Thames & Hudson, 1995).

12. Pascal Gielen, 'Institutional Imagination: Instituting Contemporary Art Minus the "Contemporary"', in *Institutional Attitudes: Instituting Art in a Flat World* (Antennae Series; 8), ed. Pascal Gielen (Amsterdam: Valiz, 2013), pp. 30–31. A couple of paragraphs prior, he proposes: 'Just as the market today is overflowing its banks, the art institution will have to go beyond its own borders and intervene in the world. It would be an illusion to think that we can keep neoliberalism from penetrating the walls of the institutions. What's more, it would be

reactionary to defensively withdraw
again to one's own temple in the spirit
of the modernist ideal. Rather, art will
have to burst at the seams and break
into "alien" social domains such as
the domestic domain of the private
home, into the familiar spheres of its
peers in art academies and studios,
into civil space and the political arena
and, yes, into the free market and
ruling neoliberalism.'

Staging Them
Entartete Kunst from Past to Present

Jonas Staal

The *Entartete Kunst* (Degenerate Art) exhibition staged by the Nazi regime, stands as a historical case study of propaganda. Its denouncement of modern art, displayed as a chamber of horrors, contributed to compose an overarching enemy figure, a fabricated threat against the construct of the 'Aryan' nation. This translated to a fundamental opposition: modern art stood for chaos, immorality and madness—for degeneracy—and this threatened the harmony, homogeneity, and racial purity of the true body politic. At the time of the first *Entartete Kunst* exhibition, the composition of this enemy figure took the form of the 'Bolshevik-Jewish' conspiracy for world governance. But in the subsequent chapters of *Entartete Kunst* showcased throughout Germany, this enemy figure of degeneracy would more emphatically come to include black peoples as well.

The aim of propaganda is not to merely send a message, but to construct reality as such: to engineer a collectively embodied 'new normal'.[1] The *Entartete Kunst* exhibition clearly fits this definition of propaganda, as it aimed to enforce a new national consent based on the dichotomy of racial purity versus degeneracy.

To construct a new reality, propaganda needs infrastructure, it needs a narrative, and it needs an imagination. In the case of Nazi Germany, this *infrastructure* consisted of the entire control over the state apparatus, which included all forms of media communication and cultural production. The *narrative*—or 'master narrative'[2] in the words of Terence McSweeney—is essentially the Nazi's origin story that tells us of its past, its present, and its desired future, which in this case is based on a mythological construction of racial purity which needs to be regained in order to defend the body politic from degeneracy and collapse. And lastly, the *imagination* that results from the Nazi's infrastructure and master narrative, relates to the creation of a thousand-year Reich, embodied by the architectural model of Germania—the new name of Berlin—designed by Hitler and architect Albert Speer.

The 'Us versus Them' dichotomy is fundamental to any propaganda to create a successful antagonism by identifying a people in relation to their shared threat. In the case of oppressive propaganda, such as that of the Nazi regime, the enemy figure is composed not of real existential threats, but of relatively easy to defeat minorities—a strategy that guarantees a quick 'heroic' success over, in this case, the Jewish people and other minorities, and in the case of many contemporary examples of resurgent authoritarianism and fascism, against Muslims and people of colour in general (often euphemistically referred to as 'migrants'). The *Entartete Kunst* exhibition succeeds, by using the Us (racial purity) versus Them (degeneracy) dichotomy to do two things at the same time: it constructs a relatively easy to defeat enemy that is trumped up as a major existential threat, while articulating through this 'negative social contract' what defines a true people.[3] In other words, not what we have in common is what defines us, but what we are threatened by—what 'they' are, 'we' are *not*.

The *Entartete Kunst* exhibition is too often described as purely historical, belonging to a bygone age of so-called 'totalitarianism'.[4] But on closer look, its narratives and strategies resonate with the culture wars in the Cold War era and today's attacks against contemporary art by ultranationalist and alt-right actors. In our 'post-modern 1930s', as Yanis Varoufakis frequently terms it, so-called cultural Marxists, genderists and globalists—with the latter structurally evoked through attacks on the Jewish-Hungarian philanthropist George Soros—are framed as a threat that aims to structurally 'depopulate' white majorities through mass migration, corrupt the nuclear family structure and sanctity of religious institutions, and weaken national sovereignty.[5] And once again, contemporary art is considered by ultranationalist and alt-right actors to embody this culture of 'degeneracy'.

I will begin this essay with an analysis of the staging of 'Them'—the composition of an enemy figure—through the use of modern art in the context of the *Entartete Kunst* exhibition, but subsequently attempt to narrate how similar strategies have continued to be employed throughout the Cold War up until the present.

1 *Entartete Kunst* Revisited

The *Entartete Kunst* exhibition that opened in Munich on 19 July 1937, was not the beginning but the culmination of an ongoing campaign against modern art waged by the Nazi regime. So-called 'Schreckenskammern der Kunst' (chambers of horror of art) or 'Schandausstellungen' (abomination exhibitions) had been structurally staged in the years preceding *Entartete Kunst*, to showcase what the Nazis considered as the 'Jewish-Bolshevist' threat. An important forerunner was *Spiegelbilder des Verfalls in der Kunst* (Images of Decadence in Art) that opened in Dresden in 1933, before travelling to eight other German cities until 1936.[6] Some years before, in the book *Kunst und Rasse* (Art and Race, 1928), Nazi architect and racial theorist Paul Schultze-Naumburg had already raged against the degeneracy of modern art set against the 'noble race' that had brought about antiquity and the Renaissance, concluding: 'Wherever a race degenerates, racial feeling has to disappear as well, and whenever racial feeling disappears, the ideal type in every genuine race is also lost.'[7] The origins of these ideas might be found already in the pseudoscience of physician and writer Max Nordau, a co-founder of the World Zionist Organization, who published his two-part treatise *Entartung* (Degeneration) in 1892–1893. Nordau perceived the early advents of modern art—from the pre-Raphaelites to the Symbolists—as part of an 'epidemic' of degeneration and hysteria, arguing that 'It never occurs to us to permit the criminal by organic disposition to "expand" his individuality in crime, and just as little can it be expected of us to permit the degenerate artist to expand his individuality in immoral works of art'.[8]

The notion of a degenerate art was thus structured on a pathological gaze long in the making in which the works of modern artists were considered direct symptoms of a time of supposed political anarchy and moral decay, compared to an idealized past of racial purity that was to be regenerated by the Nazi regime. Whereas the suffocatingly crowded 'Entartete Kunst' exhibition displayed a chaotically hung collection of works by abstract, Cubist, Expressionist and Surrealist artists, juxtaposed with photographs of physical 'deformations' and the mentally ill, a day before its opening, the *Grosse Deutsche Kunstausstellung* (Great German Art Exhibition) had been inaugurated in the pompous and spatial halls of Munich's newly constructed Haus der Deutschen Kunst (House of German Art). While works of Oskar Kokoschka and Georg Grosz in the *Entartete Kunst* exhibition exposed the brutalities of the First World War and its aftermath of poverty and mental illness, which the Nazis considered as a shaming of their national pride and sacrifice, the *Grosse Deutsche Kunstausstellung* was structured on a regressive neo-classicism where the towering muscular sculptures of Nazi-favourite Arno Breker and the clinical Aryan nudes of painter Adolf Ziegler represented the Nazi renaissance Adolf Hitler aimed to bring about. 'Germany ... means to have a *German* art once again', Hitler roared at the opening of the *Grosse Deutsche Kunstausstellung*, 'and this, like all the creative values of a people, must and will be an *eternal* art'.[9]

But the dichotomy between the supposed chaos and degeneration of modern art and an eternal racially pure art, was not yet as absolute as the Nazis claimed it to be. Expressionist painter Emil Nolde, whose works were included in *Entartete Kunst*, had been an early supporter and member of the Nazi party, and Minister of Propaganda Joseph Goebbels had made great efforts, to no avail, to convince Hitler that Nolde's 'Nordic expressionism' represented the new vitality of the Nazi regime. Some artists found their works exhibited in *both* exhibitions, such as sculptor Rudolf Belling, whose bronze sculpture of a tripod of dynamic abstracted figures titled *Dreiklang* was considered degenerate, whereas his figurative muscular figure *Der Boxer Schmeling* was deemed racially pure.[10] And while the *Entartete Kunst* exhibition framed degeneracy as inherent to their imagined Bolshevik-Jewish plot for world domination, only six of the 112 artists included were actually Jewish (instead, by displaying the purchasing price of each of the works in the inflated currency of the former Weimar Republic, which made them seem excessive, the 'Jewish' character of the works was allocated to the financialization of modern art rather than its creation).[11] But despite these contradictions, *Entartete Kunst* stood as a culminating point of the preceding chambers of horror exhibitions, in its endeavour to use art to stage a common enemy: the frightening ambiguity of 'Them' versus the monocultural construction of 'Us' in the 'Us versus Them' dichotomy.

Two million people would visit the *Entartete Kunst* exhibition, compared to the 420,000 that came to see the *Grosse Deutsche Kunstausstellung*. The affective joy of experiencing fear, rancour and superiority—comparable to visiting the carnival of rarities—became a crucial part of the Nazi propaganda arsenal. And it seems essential, in the light of the resurgence of authoritarianism and fascism in our present time, to consider how important the *pleasure principle* of fascism is. Too often, support of fascist politics is explained as a result of economic crisis and social frustrations, but the unambiguous joy that fascism offers in claiming superiority and imposing violence upon others cannot be underestimated: Pier Paolo Pasolini's *Salò o le 120 giornate di Sodoma* (*Salò, or the 120 Days of Sodom*, 1975) continues to stand as a rare and ground-breaking study into this subject.

The Nazis would continue to engage the fascist pleasure principle in subsequent exhibitions. Later in the same year, *Der ewige Jude* (The Eternal Jew) exhibition opened in Munich as well, claiming to expose the 'biological foundations of Jewry' and their aspirations for world domination. Displays consisted of chaotic photocollages that derived their vocabulary from Bolshevik poster art, re-emphasizing the overarching danger posed by the Jewish-Bolshevik enemy, but also—as Michael Tymkiw points out—pitting avant-garde 'fragmentation' versus Nazi monoculture.[12] But the exhibition also featured fairground-attraction styled chapters, such as the staging of a Jewish freemason's lodge full of skeletons. In this light, *Der ewige Jude* 'turned Jew-hating into a kind of entertainment'.[13] The success of these blockbuster exhibitions would also come to include *Entartete Musik*, which was mounted for the first time in 1938, as part of the *Reichsmusiktage* (Reich music festival). Its aim was to expose 'degenerate tonality'[14] through the works of Arnold Schoenberg as well as 'primitive' jazz.[15] Its exhibition poster depicted a black jazz musician, playing a saxophone, his jacket marked by a star of David depicted in bright socialist red. It is an image that essentially aimed to expand the Jewish-Bolshevik enemy into the Afro-Jewish-Bolshevik threat. And just as these enemy figures merged gradually through Nazi propaganda, so did these traveling blockbuster exhibitions themselves begin to mutate when *Entartete Kunst* and *Entartete Musik* merged after their respective openings into a single touring exhibition. The staging of Them solidified.

The fall of the Nazi regime is often equated with the fall of its theory on a racially pure versus a degenerate art, but already in the years following the Second World War, a new take on its practice emerged in the context of the capitalist democracy of the United States and its imperialist ambitions as embodied by the Central Intelligence Agency (CIA).

2 Reverse *Entartete Kunst*

Whereas the Nazi regime showcased modern art as the embodiment of degeneracy, after the second world war American modernist art would be employed for an equally propagandistic purpose, but would now come to represent American *supremacy*. The CIA saw the abstract works of modernist artists and their supposed 'apolitical' stance as an ideal counter-point to the overtly propagandistic neo-classicism of the Nazis as well as the Soviet doctrine of socialist realism that continued to be produced behind the Iron Curtain—despite the fact that in the United States itself, modernist art was attacked through rhetoric that had frightening resonance with that employed by the Nazis. The idea of a cultural supremacy of American modernist art thus existed mainly in the mindset of an artistic elite on one hand, and an elite of secret service members on the other. The CIA, through its front organization, the Congress for Cultural Freedom (CCF), would fund exhibitions and concerts in Europe to propagate American abstract expressionism and modern music, claiming itself as a safe haven of the cultural avant-garde in the face of the Soviets. CCF supported projects included large-scale touring exhibitions such as *Modern Art in the United States* (1955) and *The New American Painting* (1958–1959), which according to Frances Stonor Saunders, should essentially be regarded as a form of *reverse Entartete Kunst*.[16] And the scope of this reverse *Entartete Kunst* operation was vast. From 1950 until 1976 the CCF 'had offices in thirty-five countries, employed dozens of personnel, published over twenty prestige magazines, held art exhibitions, owned a news and features service, organized high profile international conferences, and rewarded musicians and artists with prizes and public performances'.[17]

Were artists and critics merely instrumentalized for the propagandistic endeavours of the CIA, or was the use of their work for political ends a continuation of their own political convictions? Art critic Clement Greenberg claimed American modern art to be a superior *modernist* art, characterized by its abstract 'purity' that was the 'guarantee of its standards of quality' as much as of its 'independence'.[18] The counter-point to modernist art was the instrumentalized 'kitsch' of dictatorships, as Greenberg argued: 'The encouragement of kitsch is merely another of the inexpensive ways in which totalitarian regimes seek to ingratiate themselves with their subjects.'[19] But this did not keep Greenberg from seeking for another kind of instrumentalization of modernist art, as he affiliated himself with the anti-communist movement. This is exemplified by his membership of the American Committee for Cultural Freedom (ACCF) in the early 1950s, an organization that campaigned against communism and was directly tied to the CCF.[20] The ACCF was symptomatic for the beginning of the Cold War and the rise of McCarthyism, that trumped up the Red Scare. Greenberg would serve as a prominent member from 1952–1953, and the level at which he sympathized with the organization's agenda is expressed by his falling-out with fellow member and historian Arthur M. Schlesinger, whom Greenberg accused of not actively pursuing anti-communist activities.[21] Greenberg was also one of the core members of the organization who refused to denounce the anti-communist campaigns of Senator McCarthy.[22]

These positions seemed, with few exceptions, widely shared by the artists Greenberg favoured. Apart from the painter Ad Reinhardt, who, unlike most abstract expressionists that had previously espoused Marxist sympathies remained loyal to his leftist political orientation, and who was the only one of the group to participate in the March on Washington in support of black rights in 1963, many of the artists had direct and voluntary links to the anti-Communist movement. Robert Motherwell and Jackson Pollock—just like Greenberg—were members of the ACCF. In 1940, Mark Rothko and Adolph Gottlieb helped to establish the Foundation of Modern Painters and Sculptors, 'which started by condemning all threats to culture from nationalistic and reactionary political movements', but in later months became an active agent in the anti-Communist movement by 'exposing Party influence in various art organizations' with the aim to 'destroy all Communist presence in the art world'.[23]

In this light, the notion of 'purity' in abstract expressionism loses its self-proclaimed 'universal' characteristics (considering the group was structured on an idea of the dominating white male genius, there was never much 'universal' to it anyway). Pollock's 'drippings' suddenly need to be evaluated in a specific geopolitical context. His wild dances around his canvasses while dripping paint in all directions are not merely an attempt to arrive at a truth located 'within' the act of painting itself, but should rather be understood as a ritual performance of the doctrine of freedom espoused by the dominant structures of power in capitalist democracy. The propagandistic strength of his work and that of the other abstract expressionists was located in the fact that while their anti-communist affiliations and intentions were explicit, their images claimed a universalism beyond the sphere of politics. In the words of art historian Eva Cockcroft, who contributed significantly to revealing the propagandistic role of modernist art in the CCF: 'the Abstract Expressionists succeeded in creating an important new art movement. They also contributed, whether they knew it or not, to a purely political phenomenon—the supposed divorce between art and politics which so perfectly served America's needs in the cold war.'[24] In our minds, the drippings of Pollock remain abstract; they do not 'depict' heroic American leaders or evil communists, even though, in fact, *they do*. In essence, there is nothing non-figurative about the works of modernist propaganda art, as it offers figurative representations of the freedom supposedly inherent to non-figurative representation. As such, it also embodies a key characteristic of propaganda art espoused by democratic regimes compared to dictatorships, namely to be visible as art, but invisible as propaganda.

Through progressive culture, the Soviet enemy could be exposed in its barbarity, both politically and culturally. But precisely here one of the great paradoxes of the CCF becomes evident, namely that its preference for modernist art was far more progressive than any other, overt national arts programme of the United States itself. For example, 'President Truman articulated a view held by many Americans that linked experimental, and especially abstract art to degenerate or subversive impulses'.[25] And under Senator McCarthy's witch hunt for Communist conspirators this sentiment was only strengthened. McCarthy's close ally, George Anthony Dondero of the US House of Representatives, even proclaimed that '[a]ll modern art is Communistic', claiming cubism, futurism, dadaism, expressionism, abstractionism, and surrealism to be 'primitive', 'insane', and 'in denial of reason'.[26]

Paradoxically, the works that supported the CIA project of a reverse *Entartete Kunst* where thus, simultaneously, rejected as degenerate. This shows that the same artwork can serve opposite goals within different propaganda narratives. Or, even more complex, that a propaganda can both communicate a particular artwork as superior *and* degenerate at the very same time, serving different publics in the process: affirming the conservatism and fascist tendencies of constituents at home, while promoting an enlightened self-image abroad. On a national level, modernist art was used to construct a 'degenerate' Bolshevik enemy figure, while in Europe, they figured as a contrast point to the 'degeneracy' of Soviet socialist realist 'kitsch'. Through the same works, two enemy figures beneficial to the overall policies of the United States were staged at the very same time.

3 *Entartete Kunst* Today

What remains today of these strategies of *Entartete Kunst* and its techniques of staging 'Them', the visualization of enemy figures that serve to delineate a pure versus a degenerate people? We can certainly observe a contemporary continuation of Cold War cultural policies when it comes to, for example, the state of

North-Korea. Exhibitions such as *The World According to Kim Jong-il*, mounted in the Kunsthal in Rotterdam in 2004 before travelling internationally with the catchphrase 'Never before shown North-Korean art', displayed *Juche*-styled socialist realist paintings depicting joyous peasants, heroic soldiers, and the fatherly figure of the late Kim Jong-il and his father, Kim Il-sung.[27] The exhibition's design mimicked cliché-images of agitprop displays through bold all-caps titles and walls painted red, creating a contemporary version of the chamber of horrors in which supposedly enlightened democratic citizens could look with pity and contempt upon the poor subjects of archaic Communism and their manufactured world of lies and deceit. Such exhibitions have very little to do with North-Korean art, but rather serve as a contrasting point to declare the superiority of democratic free expression.[28] In other words, rather than being displayed as propaganda for the North-Korean regime, they are displayed as propaganda for what democracy *is not*. While refraining from the discourse on degeneracy, it is nonetheless clear that such exhibitions employ a dichotomy between free democracy and oppressive dictatorship, which overlap—for a different ideological purpose—with the core mechanisms of the original *Entartete Kunst* exhibition.

Another contemporary take on *Entartete Kunst* can be found in the curious project titled the Freethinkers' Space, the first-ever exhibition space created in Dutch parliament in the political offices of the conservative-liberal People's Party for Freedom and Democracy (VVD) and the ultranationalist Freedom Party (PVV), from 2008 to 2010.[29] Exceptionally, the exhibition space was both initiated and curated by political representatives of both parties, namely the current prime minister of the Netherlands Mark Rutte for the VVD, and the second on the list of the PVV, Fleur Agema, who herself had studied architecture and was the author of an alternative prison model.[30] The starting point of the Freethinkers' Space was formed in the aftermath of the murder of right-wing polemicist and filmmaker Theo van Gogh in 2004 by Mohammed Bouyeri, member of the Islamic fundamentalist organization known as the Hofstad Group. This act of existential censorship in the form of the murder of an artist created a new cultural frame for the extreme right, who began to manically identify any cultural repression that could be interpreted as a form of censorship motivated by Islamic faith. The racist and anti-left cartoons of Gregorius Nekschot for example, which were met by online threats, became a cornerstone of right-wing cultural offensive. Even complaints by a citizen, supposedly of Muslim faith, in the village of Huizen regarding a painting of nudes titled *Danseuses Exotiques* by amateur artist Ellen Vroegh displayed in the town hall, became frontpage news for right-wing newspapers. And so, the indignation felt at a murder was transposed to isolated incidents, on which the VVD and PVV capitalized by claiming that the left-wing elite and its cultural institutions were uncapable —and unwilling—to defend enlightened free artistic expression.

In July 2008, the Freethinkers' Space was opened, including works of Theo van Gogh, Nekschot and Vroegh, establishing a new cornerstone of the Dutch culture wars. The Freethinkers' Space employs the degenerate art trope in yet another way: by showing what the supposedly 'coward' leftist cultural institutions were unwilling to, it aimed to expose the 'degeneracy' of the ruling cultural elite that was unwilling to step up to defend the freedom of speech of white 'autochthonous' citizens. Quickly, Tofik Dibi, at the time a representative of the Green Party, challenged the curators of the Freethinkers' Space to also include artworks that had been subjected to right-wing censorship, such as an image of Anne Frank wearing a Palestinian *keffiyeh* shawl by graffiti artist T., and a banned poster made by the International Socialists that depicted an image of PVV leader Wilders on a Marlboro cigarette package, including a warning for the damage to the national health his right-wing rhetoric posed. The VVD party immediately accepted this proposal, and claimed the Freethinkers' Space defended the freedom of speech no matter its political orientation—despite the evidently anti-Islamic agenda displayed upon its opening. But their co-curators of the PVV refused, as they claimed the Freethinkers' Space was dedicated to artworks faced with Islamic censorship. As a result, the Freethinkers' Space turned into a kind of ideological chessboard. The PVV left its position as co-curator, while the Green Party joined in, and with each new addition of artworks the cultural conceptualization of 'freedom' represented by the works of art changed. In this light, Dibi's intervention can be regarded as an attempt to create a counter-propaganda by undermining the Us versus Them dichotomy that attempts to impose a monocultural regime structured on white freedom of expression at the cost of everyone else, and forcing new juxtapositions and ambiguities in the way we conceptualize freedom politically, culturally and artistically.[31]

Despite such interventions, the Dutch culture war has continued to be dominated by right-wing forces. The rise of amateur pianist Thierry Baudet's ultranationalist, misogynist, and racist Forum for Democracy (FvD) party, is symptomatic in that regard, as he calls for a new cultural offensive in the form of what he calls a 'renaissance movement', exemplified by his victory speech after becoming the largest political party in the Dutch European elections of 2019:

> And so, we stand here, tonight, literally at the eleventh hour. In the midst of the debris of what was once the greatest and most beautiful civilization that the world had ever known. A civilization that encompassed every corner of the world, that was full of self-confidence, and that produced the most beautiful architecture, the most beautiful music, and the most beautiful paintings that have ever existing beneath our celestial skies. Our country is part of the civilized family.[32]

Notoriously, in the speech Baudet claims that the 'boreal world' is under threat—a term that means as much as 'far north' and is popular in extreme-right circles to claim 'white indigeneity'—due to a 'death cult' of self-hatred of the ruling elite, those who 'receive our art subsidies and design our buildings', declaring his own party to be the 'flagship of the renaissance fleet' instead.[33] In Baudet's essay 'Der "neue Mensch" ist ein Irrtum' (The New Man is an error) for the right-wing Swiss *Weltwoche* magazine, he even returns to attacking the Dadaists as an embodiment of the chaos and dangers of French Revolution ideals of radical equality, resulting in the 'ramblings' of Dadaist sound poems, and he further has openly called for the destruction of modernist buildings and propagated his disdain for atonal music.[34] As a counterpoint, Baudet—who in the meantime has become part of the art commission of Dutch parliament—demands: 'We want to recognize ourselves in the portraits of our ancestors in museums, we want to maintain our national holidays, and sing our songs and honour our history', positing this conceptualization of national culture as 'rooted' compared to the 'unrooted' nature of the cosmopolitan elite—an argument also used against the Jewish people by the Nazis.[35] It needs little historical effort to see how the dichotomy between pure and degenerate art is being replicated here: hatred of ambiguity and the desire for the monocultural order. Baudet returns full circle to the core methodology of *Entartete Kunst*.

Evidently, the Netherlands does not stand by itself in this return to the trope of degenerate art. Bjoern Hoecke, representative of the far-right Alternative for Germany (AfD), remarked on Peter Eisenman's holocaust memorial in Berlin titled *Denkmal für die ermordeten Juden Europas* (Memorial to the murdered Jews of Europe), that Germans were the 'only people in the world who planted a memorial of shame in the heart of their capital'.[36] And the newly government-appointed director of the Ujazdowski Castle in Warsaw, Piotr Bernatowicz, has announced a battle against the art institutions that he considers to 'look like left-wing ideological ghettos', instantly cancelling collaborations with projects such as the Anti-Fascist Year.[37] Bernatowicz considers 'cultural Bolshevism' to dominate contemporary art production, which he wishes to combat—phrasings that are literally included in the institution's policy plan for the coming years.[38] Pride instead of shame in the face of national histories, however violent and cruel—or exactly *because* of the fascist pleasure principle that is derived from violence and cruelty—against the chaos, multiculturalism and gender-confusion supposedly propagated by cultural Bolshevism or, more popular, 'cultural Marxism': this rhetoric and these developments clearly articulate a new paradigm of degenerate versus pure art manifesting in our present time. The *Entartete Kunst* exhibition never entirely closed.

But this desperate return to monocultural paradigms, embodied by authoritarians from Trump to Bolsonaro, from Erdogan to Modi, also face a new *ambiguity politics*, that propagates not the staging of a fictional enemy but addresses real existential crises instead. The colonial and white supremacist statues that are being toppled and modified at this very moment as a result of the transformative Black Lives Matter movement, despite the desperate attempts of monocultural protagonists to maintain them as cornerstones for a renewed white 'renaissance'; the demands for pluri-historical canons that narrate not an absolute 'People' but *peoples-in-the-making*; and the role that artists play in new transnational movements and platforms, from the Democracy in Europe 2025 Movement (DiEM25) to the Progressive International to contribute to imagining new models of egalitarian life forms—these examples show a new insurgent emancipatory politics coming into being. Unlike the oppressive propagandas we

discussed so far, such popular mass movements seek new forms of interdependent storytelling. They do not approach the past nostalgically, but the present transformatively; and the futures it proposes are not given but to be authored collectively in the process. Common infrastructures, common narratives, common imaginations—these do not represent top-down manipulative engineering, but a collective practice of world-making. In the face of monocultural propagandas, such emancipatory propagations—the propagation of ambiguity politics enabling a new pluricultural composition of *Us*—are a vital force to overcome the false dichotomies imposed upon us in violent pasts and presents.

Notes

1   I base this notion of propaganda as
a performance of power that aims to
construct reality—rather than merely
communicate within a given reality—
on, amongst others, the propaganda
model of Noam Chomsky and
Edward S. Herman, *Manufacturing
Consent* (New York: Pantheon Books,
1988). See for further elaboration,
Jonas Staal, *Propaganda Art in the
21st Century* (Cambridge, MA, and
London: MIT Press, 2019).

2   Terence McSweeney, *The 'War on
Terror' and American Film: 9/11 Frames
Per Second* (Edinburgh University
Press, 2016), p. 10.

3   This notion of a 'negative social
contract' I take from Joseph Masco,
The Theater of Operations (Durham
and London: Duke University Press,
2014), p. 48.

4   Slavoj Žižek, *Did Someone Say
Totalitarianism?* (London and New
York: Verso, 2001).

5   See for an extensive mapping of the
contemporary culture wars, Sven
Lütticken, 'Performing Culture
Otherwise', in Sven Lütticken and
Maria Hlavajova, eds., *Propositions for
Non-Fascist Living: Deserting from the
Culture Wars* (London, Cambridge,
MA, and Utrecht: MIT Press and
BAK, basis voor actuele kunst, 2020),
pp. 5-35. See also: Sven Lütticken,
'Cultural Marxists Like Us', *Afterall* 46
(Autumn/Winter 2018).

6   Christoph Zuschlag, 'An
"Educational" Exhibition: The
Precursors of Entartete Kunst and
Its Individual Venues', in Stephanie
Barron, ed., *Entartete Kunst: The Fate
of the Avant-Garde in Nazi Germany*
(New York: Harry N. Abrams, 1991),
pp. 83-97.

7   Paul Schultze-Naumburg, 'Art and
Race', in Anton Kaes, Martin Jay
and Edward Dimendberg, eds., *The
Weimar Republic Sourcebook* (Berkeley,
Los Angeles and London: University
of California Press, 1994), pp. 496-
499, 498.

8   Max Nordau, *Degeneration* (New York:
D. Appleton and Company, 1895), p.
326.

9   Facsimile of the *Entartete Kunst*
exhibition brochure in Barron, ed.,
'Entartete Kunst', pp. 356-390, 366.

10   Mario-Andreas von Luttichau,
'Entartete Kunst, Munich 1973: A
Reconstruction', in ibid., pp. 45-81,
55.

11   Stephanie Barron, '1937 Modern Art
and Politics in Prewar Germany', in
ibid., pp. 9-23, 9. de Mello in 1992.

12   Michael Tymkiw, *Nazi Exhibition
Design and Modernism* (Minneapolis
and London: University of Minnesota
Press, 2018), pp. 169-219.

13   Ibid., p. 172.

14   Zuschlag, 'An Educational Exhibition',
in Barron, ed., 'Entartete Kunst', p. 95.

15   Michael Meyer, 'A Musical Façade for
the Third Reich', ibid., pp. 171-183,
171.

16   Frances Stonor Saunders, *Who Paid
the Piper: The CIA and the Cultural
Cold War* (London: Granta Books,
2000), p. 119.

17   Ibid., p. 1.

18   Clement Greenberg, *Art and Culture:
Critical Essays* (Boston: Beacon Press,
1989), p. 755.

19   Ibid., p. 19.

20   Nancy Jachec, 'Modernism,
Enlightenment Values, and Clement
Greenberg', *Oxford Art Journal* 21, no.
2 (1998), pp. 123-132.

21   Ibid., p. 172.

22   Saunders, *Who Paid the Piper*, p. 199.

23   Ibid., pp. 275-277.

24   Eva Cockcroft, 'Abstract
Expressionism, Weapon of the Cold
War', *Artforum* 12, no. 10 (June 1974),
pp. 39-41.

25   Saunders, *Who Paid the Piper*, p. 252.

26   Ibid., p. 253.

27   Often translated as 'self-reliance',
Juche is the translation of Marxism-
Leninism by Kim Il-sung into the
specific conditions of North-Korea,
with strong emphasis on self-defence
and national independence.

28   For a less propagandistic study of
North-Korean art production, I refer
to the work of Jane Portal. Although
keeping in line with the problematic
general characterization of North-
Korea as 'totalitarian', she also maps
the broader aesthetic vocabulary in
North Korean art and crafts, among
others in the form of traditional
contemporary landscapes in coloured
ink, glass, and porcelain works, and
the curious and undertheorized
practice of painterly depictions
of antiquities and archaeological
findings. See: Jane Portal, *Art Under
Control in North Korea* (London:
Reaktion Books, 2005).

29   See for a full documentation of the

Freethinkers' Space history and artworks, Jonas Staal, *Art Property of Politics II: Freethinkers' Space* (Eindhoven: Van Abbemuseum, 2010).

30 See further Jonas Staal, *Art, Property of Politics III: Closed Architecture* (Eindhoven: Onomatopee, 2011).

31 Together with the Van Abbemuseum in Eindhoven, I reconstructed the Freethinkers' Space in 2010 in the museum as a case-study of the role of art in contemporary right-wing propaganda. From 2012 onwards, in collaboration with curators Nick Aikens and Christiane Berndes, we also invited other political parties to curate their own Freethinkers' Space in a project titled 'Freethinkers' Space Continued', to expand on the 'ideological chessboard' that the Freethinkers' Space became after Dibi's intervention and counter the right-wing cultural paradigm. The Green Party and social-liberal Democrats 66 (D66) curated their spaces in the Van Abbemuseum, the Labour Party in De Appel arts centre in Amsterdam, and the Socialist Party in cultural centre kuS in Heerlen.

32 Original quote: 'En zo staan we hier vanavond. Te elfder ure, letterlijk. Te midden van de brokstukken van wat ooit de grootste en mooiste beschaving was die de wereld ooit heeft gekend. Een beschaving die alle uithoeken van de wereld bestreek, die vol zelfvertrouwen was, en die de mooiste architectuur, de mooiste muziek en de mooiste schilderkunst heeft voortgebracht die ooit onder de sterrenhemel heeft bestaan. Ons land maakt onderdeel uit van die beschavingsfamilie.' Transcription of Baudet's victory speech, 20 March 2019.

33 Ibid.

34 Thierry Baudet, 'Der "neue Mensch" ist ein Irrtum', *Die Weltwoche*, 24 July 2019.

35 Original quote: 'We willen onszelf herkennen in de portretten van onze voorvaderen in onze musea, we willen onze feestdagen behouden, onze liederen zingen en onze geschiedenis eren', Paul Steenhuis, 'Baudets probleem met Beethoven (en de vernielers van de "boreale" cultuur)', *NRC Handelsblad*, 7 August 2019.

36 Katrin Bennhold and Melissa Eddy, '"Hitler or Höcke?" Germany's Far-Right Party Radicalizes', *New York Times*, 26 October 2019.

37 Robert Stasinski, 'Ujazdowski Castle Takes a Right-Wing Turn', *Kunstkritikk*, 16 March 2020. https://kunstkritikk.com/ujazdowski-castle-takes-a-right-wing-turn/.

38 Ibid.

Following the Exhibition, National Collection

Public Movement

Imagine this museum is a country,

and in this country there is a museum.

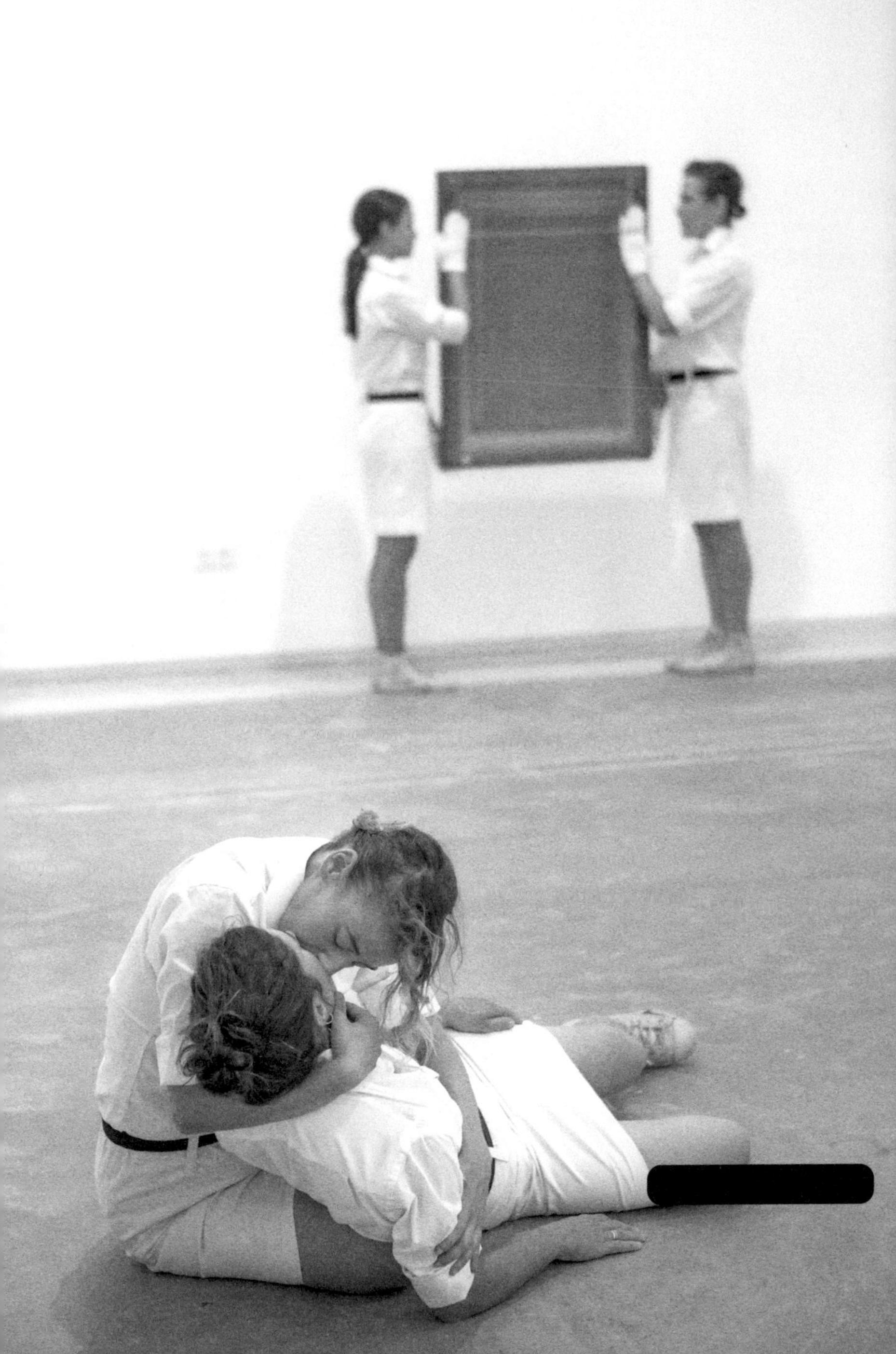

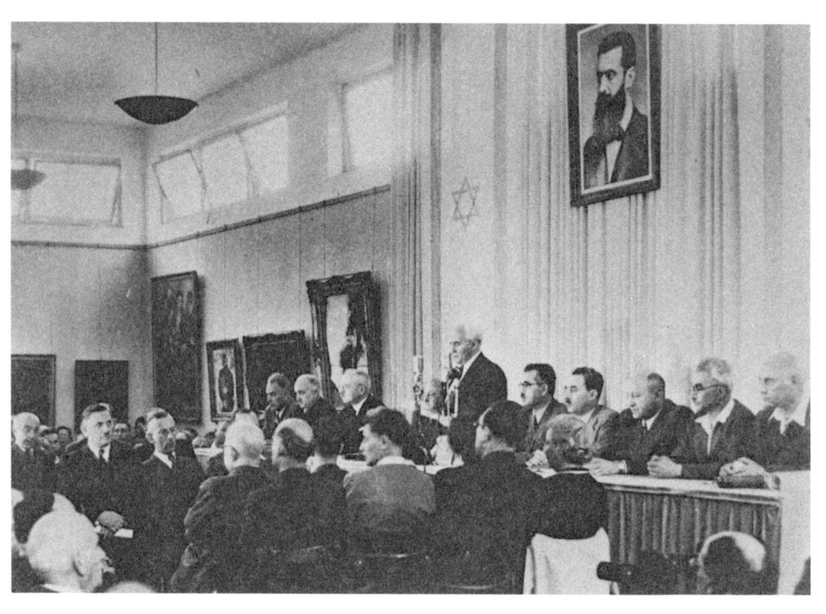

The Aesthetics of Ambiguity

72

ON THE 14TH OF MAY, 1948, THE DECLARATION OF THE STATE OF ISRAEL WAS STAGED IN THE MAIN GALLERY OF THE TEL AVIV MUSEUM OF ART. DURING THOSE FIRST FEW YEARS OF THE STATE, THE MUSEUM SERVED AS A PUBLIC ART SPACE BY DAY, AND A PARLIAMENTARY HALL BY NIGHT. THE PERFORMANCE OF POLITICS THAT TOOK PLACE IN THE 'HALL OF ART' SET THE FOUNDATION FOR A COMPLEX AND LONG-STANDING INTERDEPENDENCY BETWEEN THE NATION-STATE AND ITS CULTURAL INSTITUTIONS.

IN DECEMBER 2015, MEMBERS OF PUBLIC MOVEMENT
CARRIED THE PAINTING 'HOLSTEIN SWITZERLAND' BY
URY LESSER IN A PROCESSIONAL CEREMONY FROM THE
ORIGINAL MUSEUM SITE TO THE NEW TEL AVIV MUSEUM
OF ART. THEY INSTALLED THE PAINTING THERE, AND
IN DOING SO, COMPLETED THEIR RECONSTRUCTION OF
THE INDEPENDENCE HALL TO ONCE AGAIN HIGHLIGHT A
SET OF RELATIONSHIPS BETWEEN THE NATION-STATE
AND ITS MUSEUMS.

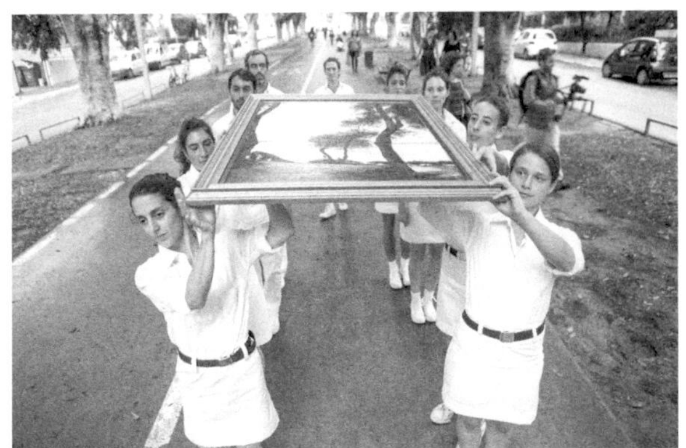

Rothschild Boulevard, Tel Aviv

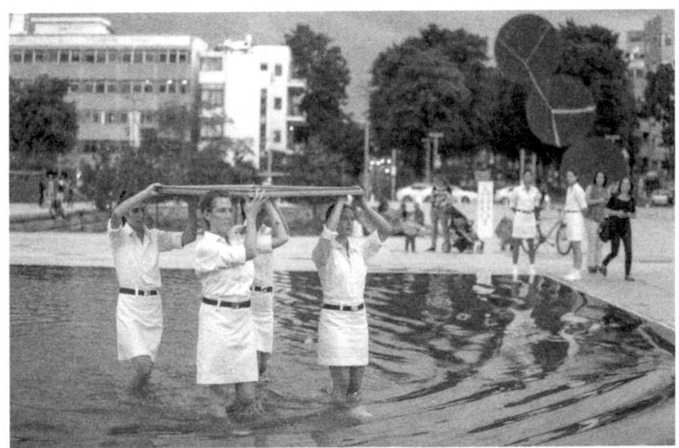

Habima Square ('The Square of Culture'), Tel Aviv

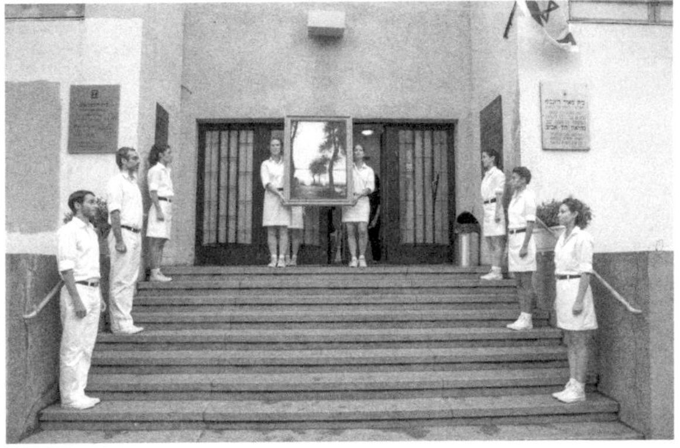

Independence Hall, 16 Rothschild Boulevard, Tel Aviv

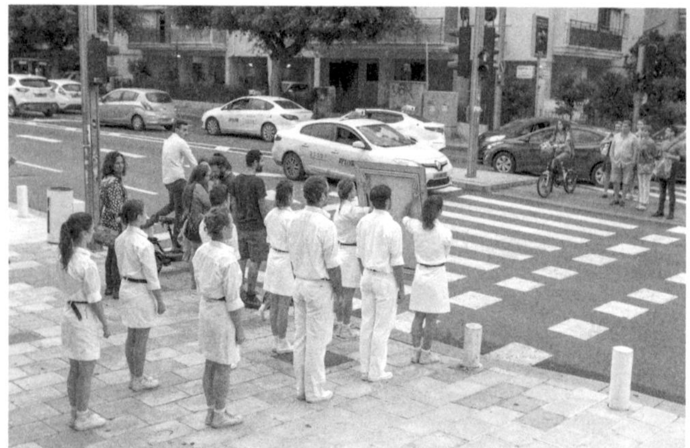

Cross Road next to Helena Rubinstein Pavilion for Contemporary Art, Tel Aviv

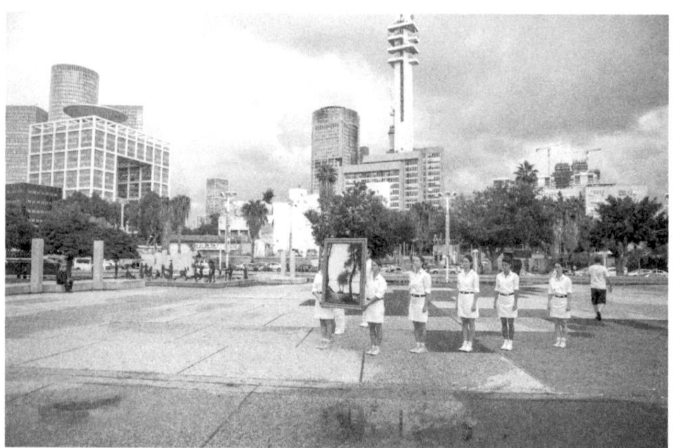

Facing the Tel Aviv Museum of Art. Behind: Camp Rabin military base

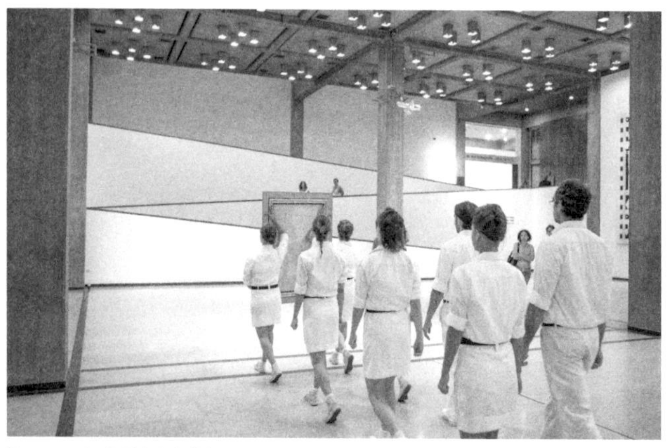

Entrance hall, Tel Aviv Museum of Art

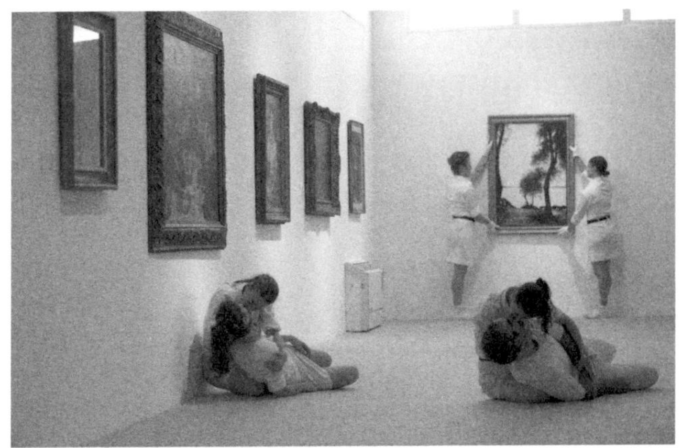

Reconstructed interior of the Independence Hall, Tel Aviv Museum of Art

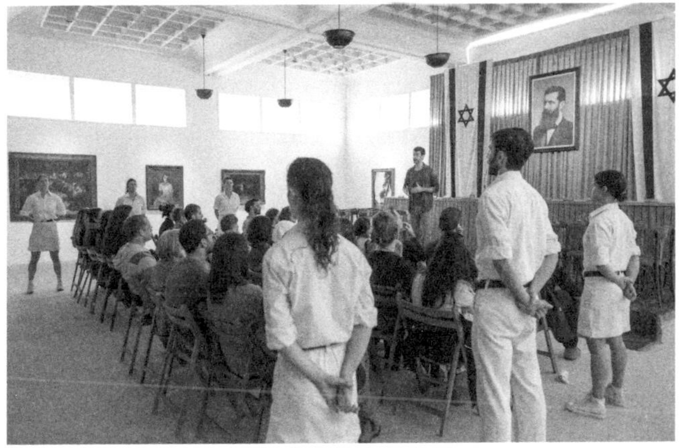

WE'RE ASSAMBLED IN HEAVY CONCRETE,
MOVING LIGHTLY THROUGH SILENT GALLERIES.
WORKS OF ART ARE AT REST.
HERE THEY ACCUMILATE.
FOREVER.

WE ARE SURROUNDED BY MOVEMENT.

ARTWORKS ARE BEING PACKED AND UNPACKED,
LENT,
INSURED,
SHIPPED AND RETURNED,
CATALOGED,
STORED, RESTORED AND PRESERVED.

THE BELLY OF THE MUSEUM PULLS INWARD.

WE SERVE A PURPOSE.
THERE IS A VOID BETWEEN US.
THERE ARE ARTWORKS THAT WILL NEVER BE CARRIED
THROUGH THIS HALL,
A NON-NATIONAL COLLECTION.

IMAGINE THIS MUSEUM IS A COUNTRY,
AND IN THIS COUNTRY THERE IS A MUSEUM.

The Aesthetics of Ambiguity

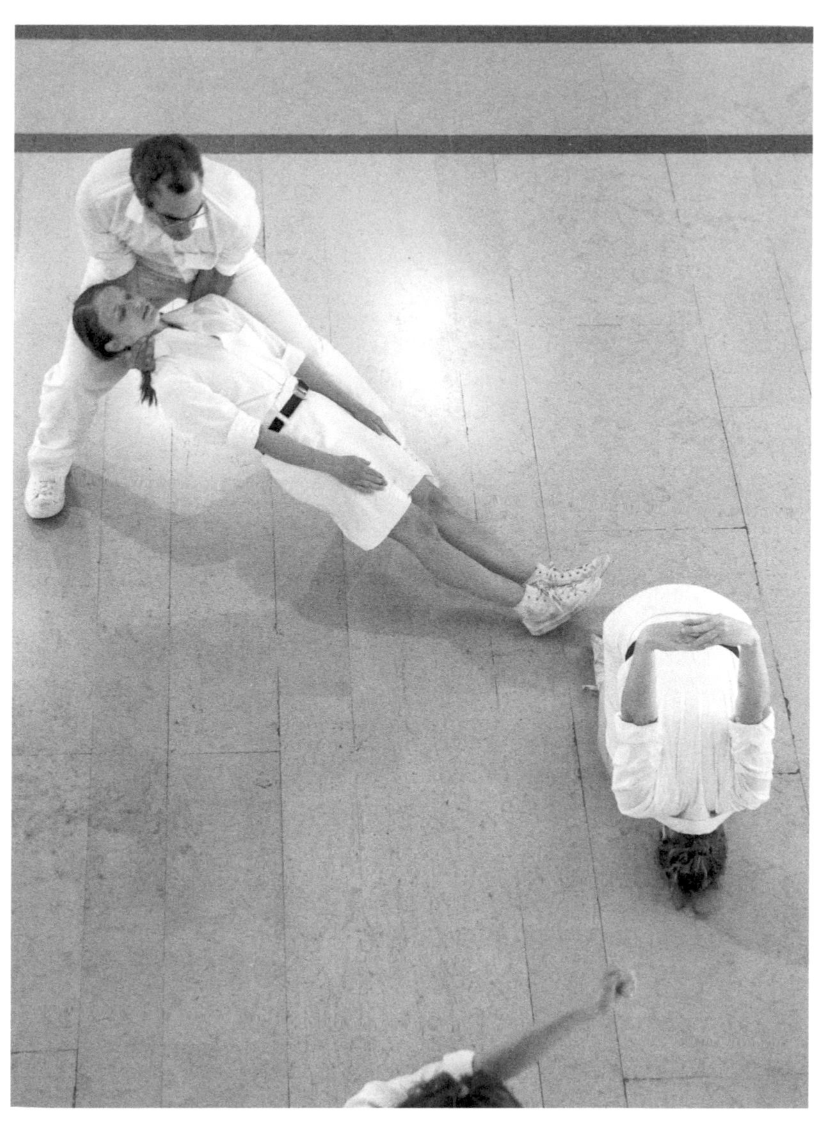

Public Movement

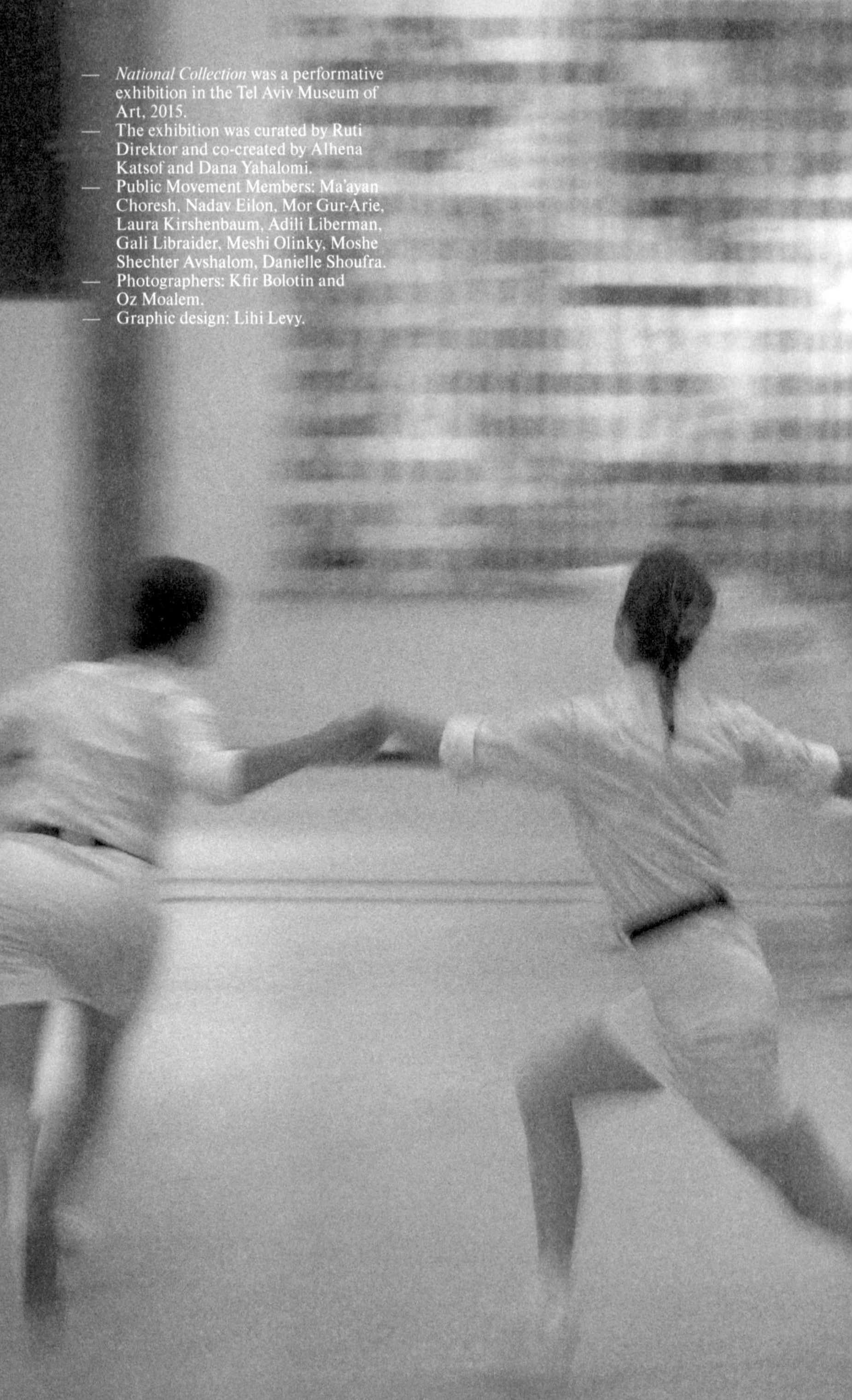

— *National Collection* was a performative exhibition in the Tel Aviv Museum of Art, 2015.
— The exhibition was curated by Ruti Direktor and co-created by Alhena Katsof and Dana Yahalomi.
— Public Movement Members: Ma'ayan Choresh, Nadav Eilon, Mor Gur-Arie, Laura Kirshenbaum, Adili Liberman, Gali Libraider, Meshi Olinky, Moshe Shechter Avshalom, Danielle Shoufra.
— Photographers: Kfir Bolotin and Oz Moalem.
— Graphic design: Lihi Levy.

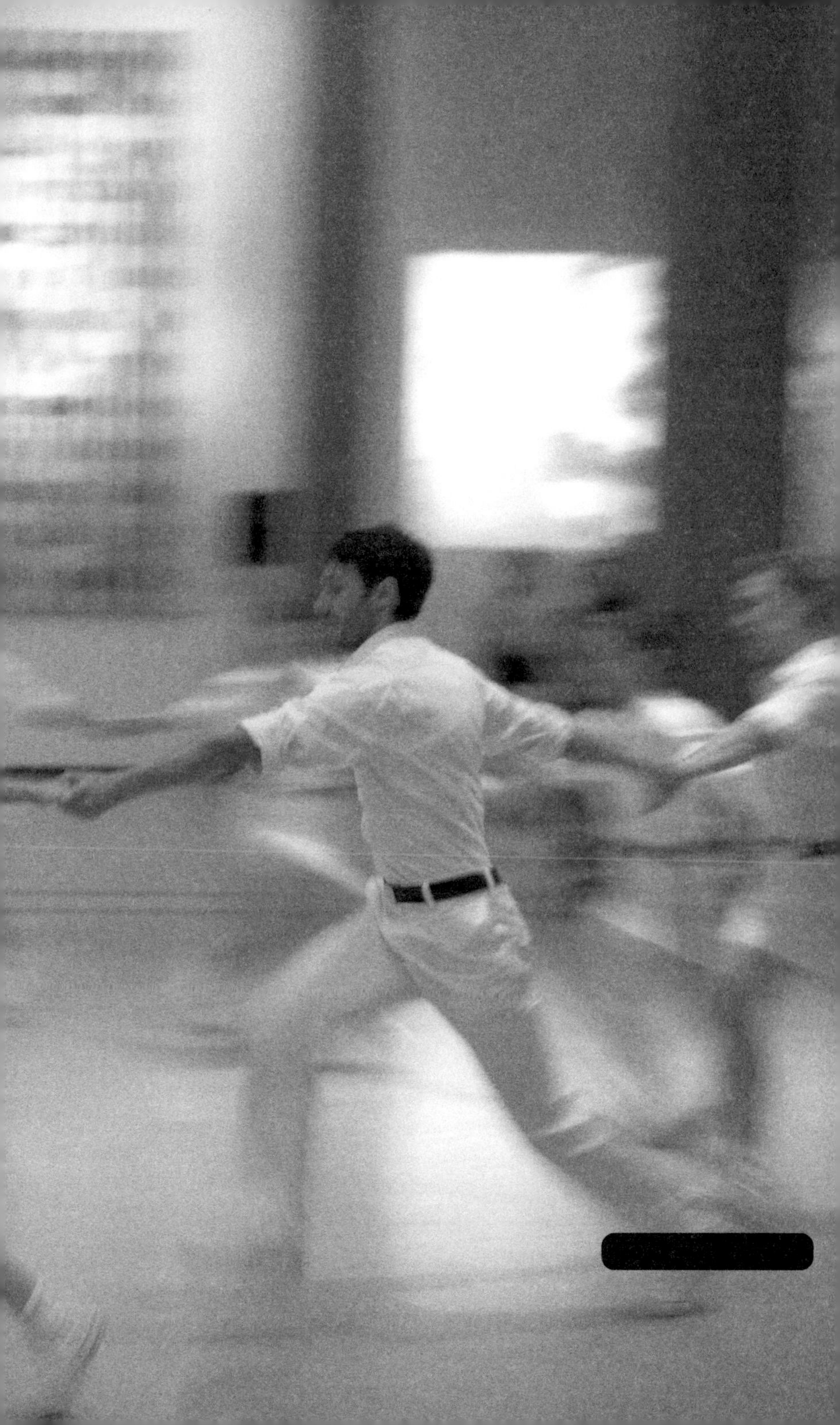

Settler Capitalist Multiculturalism, Indigenous Refusal, and the Spectre of Bankruptcy
Rebecca Belmore's 'Gone Indian'

Max Haiven

The tension between monocultures and multiculturalism, and the role of ambiguity in that relationship can be fruitfully explored by examining the work of celebrated Anishinaabe[1] performance artist Rebecca Belmore in which she responds to the ambiguities and complexities of Indigenous presence and resistance in the territories currently known as Canada. In this chapter, I provide a reading on Belmore's 2009 performance *Gone Indian*, which took place outside the headquarters of the nation's largest bank in the heart of Toronto's financial district. The piece indexes the radical Indigenous refusal of inclusion within the hegemony of Canadian 'settler capitalist' multiculturalism,[2] a reflection or refraction of ongoing Indigenous activist struggles against Canada's ongoing colonial agenda of eliminating Indigenous presence on land to make way for the financially-driven extractive and logistics industries that are pivotal to the nation's political economy. This elimination sometimes takes the form of direct violence (police repression), sometimes of indirect violence (poverty) and sometimes of 'predatory inclusion' within the dominant political and economic frameworks of the nation-state which nonetheless seek to eliminate Indigenous people as an autonomous and, importantly, land-based sovereign people.

Liberal and conservative commentators have maligned Indigenous protests, in both the political-economic and the artistic realm, as monocultural defensiveness out of step with multicultural realities, an immature (even self-defeating) attachment to tradition and an unrealistic demand for the recognition of a long-extinguished sovereignty.[3] But Belmore's hauntological work in *Gone Indian* reminds us that much more is at stake. This example, and the broader struggles against Canadian capitalist settler colonialism, indicate that it's not so much that monoculturalism and multiculturalism are endlessly opposed, but that struggles emerge around how these two notions articulate. On the one hand, the Canadian state is eager (some might say desperate) to 'include' diverse Indigenous cultures *within* a liberalist multiculturalist capitalist framework in which many monocultures might exist under *pax capitalis*: the overarching rule of financialized neoliberalism. On the other hand, Belmore's intervention, while it (like Indigenous blockades and protests) might be read as an expression of monocultural protectionism, is actually an invitation to reimagine what multiculturalism might mean, the kinds of engagements, relationships, kinships, and political formations that might have been possible and might yet be possible 'underneath' settler colonial capitalism. To do so, Belmore uses money and debt as motifs, as well as a hauntological strategy of calling up and out to ghosts: ghosts of what was, ghosts of what is, and ghosts of what might yet be on these lands.

'Gone Indian'

It's after midnight and a million people, many of them inebriated, ramble through downtown Toronto's financial district on a warm September night.[4] As they make their way between the charismatic art installations of the 2009 edition of the city's Nuit Blanche all-night public arts festival, some encounter a dilapidated and muddy burgundy van, a set of deer antlers affixed to its hood, its roof covered in an embroidered buckskin rug with a couple of old armchairs secured on top, as it drives slowly through the streets blaring Indigenous pow-wow music (drumming and singing) from a large sound-system. Eventually, the van pulled up on the curb at the headquarters to the Royal Bank of Canada, one of the world's largest financial institutions whose imposing two-tower edifice is literally made of gold infused into its glistening sheet-glass siding.[5] A crowd gathered, most of them non-Indigenous, to watch *Gone Indian*, a performance by Rebecca Belmore, perhaps Canada's best-known and most celebrated Indigenous performance artists.[6] The title was a sly pun: the 'Indian' is gone from these lands, eliminated to make room for the bustling financial district and larger city; but 'going Indian' was also a phrase used to describe European 'settlers' who developed what were perceived to be unhealthy attachments to the place and its people, being adopted into Indigenous communities or otherwise abandoning what the British called 'civility' for 'savage' ways.[7]

Belmore's performance was layered and ambiguous, blending Anishinaabe, Cree, and settler symbolism. Near the outset, Belmore, barefoot and wearing feather-adorned army-green coveralls and a black toque, placed several red cloth bags full of Canadian pennies at the periphery of the performance space and later cut them open with a knife, spilling the coins onto the sidewalk before tying the torn red fabrics to her ankle (red fabric is customarily used to wrap sacred objects). Meanwhile, celebrated Cree actor and dancer Michael Greyeyes, dressed in full pow-wow regalia, performed a series of choreographed modern dance routines, first to an Indigenous hip-hop track, next to a recording of pow-wow drumming and singing.[8] While Greyeyes' movements referenced pow-wow dancing, they were original contemporary compositions, often exhibiting jerky, halting motions as if his body were at times possessed and/or constrained by unseen, disquieting forces. The whole performance was quietly overseen and occasionally photographed by a silent Indigenous man conspicuously wearing dress pants, a white collared shirt, a black tie, a black fringed buckskin jacket, and sunglasses (despite it being nighttime), appearing as if a not-so-secret state or corporate agent. As the performance unfolded, Belmore, on her knees, used what appeared to be a heavy traditional stone mortar and pestle to attempt to grind the pennies as one might do to corn or medicines to produce an edible or healing powder. The performance ended with Greyeyes drifting, as if in slow-motion, through the space and Belmore giving up on her impossible task. The pennies remained scattered on the ground and the company drove away in the van.

This piece was intentionally ambiguous in part because, to my mind, it attempted to haunt the colonial imagination precisely at the fraught intersection where, drawing on the work of Sherene Razack, space meets place in a colonial settler state:[9] in this case the site where Indigenous land has been turned into a zone of financial speculation.

Belmore's work has been particularly important, given that she has become one of Canada's most celebrated contemporary Indigenous artists in spite of her unflinching critiques of settler colonial structural and direct violence, often with a focus on its gendered nature that targets Indigenous women, girls and Two Spirit people.[10] Her selection by the Canadian government to represent the nation at the 2005 Venice Biennale, her many shows and retrospectives at prominent Canadian cultural and international arts institutions, as well as her inclusion in many large festivals (most recently documenta 14) speaks not only to her talents as an artist but also to the vitality of Indigenous creative practices today. Canada's celebration of this work is itself ambiguous, and the nation-state's eagerness to associate itself with it (for instance, at Venice) is paradoxical, but, as I will argue, strives in part to send a message that only in so secure a multicultural capitalist democracy as Canada is such internal critique possible and welcome. Still, Belmore's work is deeply radical, on a fundamental level by using the vehicle of contemporary art, a genre prized for its 'presentness' and 'reflexivity', as a means to implicitly and explicitly refuse the racist categorization of Indigenous people as trapped in an endless rehearsal of monocultural atavism.

It has long been a technique of colonialism to identify the Indigenous or non-Western 'others' as benighted 'prehistorical' people, locked in totalizing monocultures, incapable of a reflexive impulse.[11] These others' cloistered intolerance for cultural ambiguity is taken as evidence of their unfitness for full political participation or inclusion within the body politic and justifies their oppression, subordination, and exploitation. Eurocentric notions of multiculturalism typically erase or ignore the many and diverse non-Western traditions of cosmopolitanism, tolerance, and multicultural exchange, including those international and intercultural practices and networks that existed on Turtle Island (North America) before the invasion of Europeans.[12]

Belmore's work, then, strives not to defend or shore up an Indigenous monoculture but, rather, to alert us to the spectral presence of other possibilities for intercultural encounter, and to the limits of the multicultural norm under which her audience is gathered, in the shadow of the nation's largest bank.

In the Shadow of Genocide

For readers outside of Canada, some brief facts about Canada's about the Indigenous people in that nation may be helpful. In the 2016 census, about 1.6 million people in Canada self-identified as Indigenous in one of three distinct groups: First Nations, Metis (of both Indigenous and Settler heritage) and Inuit (Indigenous to largely arctic areas). Of those self-identifying as First Nations, only three-quarters are acknowledged and registered as such by the Canadian government, largely because, over the generations, it has been official Government policy to strip Indigenous people of their status in order to assimilate them into the broader body politic. The Canadian government officially recognizes 634 distinct 'First Nations' governments in Canada with limited and highly scrutinized self-governance over small, fragmented territories (reservations) allotted and overseen by the Canadian government. Slightly less than half of all First Nations people make their primary residence in these communities, the other half living in other towns and cities. There are many Indigenous communities that are not recognized by the Canadian government, and the sovereignty of both recognized and unrecognized communities over assigned or the wider traditionally-held lands (in sum, practically the entirety of 'Canada') is not substantively acknowledged by Canada, leading to numerous conflicts. Recognized reservations constitute less than 1 per cent of land in Canada and are, simply put, economically and politically dependent on the Canadian government.[13] Most are characterized by what the UN and major human rights NGOs characterize as 'third world conditions'.

Many Indigenous people participate fully in the overarching Canadian society and represent many of the nation's luminary legal, political, cultural, academic, and business professionals. Many Indigenous people practice various forms of traditional economic, social, and cultural tradition, either as a part of their identity or community or (though it has been rendered almost impossible) as a complete way of life. These practices differ widely between distinct nations. Yet in aggregate Indigenous people, especially those living on reservations, suffer catastrophic oppression, indexed by shocking health and social indicators. In 2011 the Assembly of First Nations, the (highly moderate) confederacy of Indigenous governments recognized by the Canadian state reported that

> One in four children in First Nation communities live in poverty... almost double the national average. Suicide rates among First Nation youth are five to seven times higher than [among] other young non-Aboriginal Canadians. The life expectancy of First Nation citizens is five to seven years less than [that of] other non-Aboriginal Canadians and infant mortality rates are 1.5 times higher. Tuberculosis rates among First Nation citizens living on-reserve are 31 times the national average. A First Nation youth is more likely to end up in jail than to graduate high school. First Nation children, on average, receive 22% less funding for child welfare services than other Canadian children. There are almost 600 unresolved cases of missing and murdered Aboriginal women in Canada... In 2006, the unemployment rate for First Nation people living on-reserve was 25%—approximately three times the rate for non-Aboriginal Canadians [and] the average household income for First Nations living on-reserve was $15,958, compared to $36,000 (before taxes) for non-Aboriginal Canadians.[14]

There is a wide diversity of political opinion and debate within

Indigenous communities, and in Canada as a whole, about how these indicators might be improved. While some are keen to offer neoliberal narratives that stress the need to make Indigenous people more active participants in the dominant capitalist paradigm, there is an increasing militancy among Indigenous people towards the reclamation of lands stolen by colonialism and a resurgence of lifeways and practices that colonialism actively sought to obliterate.[15] While sometimes this resistance and resurgence takes place in the realms of education, culture, and mainstream politics, increasingly it is taking the form of active and often militant refusal of Canadian government and corporate interference on both reserve and much broader traditional Indigenous lands.[16]

Today, Indigenous protests represent the gravest internal 'threat' to Canada's pivotal extractive and logistics industries. These industries have long been central to Canada's economic vitality; these sectors are, indeed, its *raison d'etre*.[17] Much of the area that is now claimed by Canada was once ruled by a private corporation, the Hudson's Bay Company, a state-chartered British monopoly whose business was the extraction of furs and timber. The nation's birth as an independent state was only possible with the building of railways, allowed both for extracted resources of the interior to be brought to Atlantic ports and for European settlers to be shipped West to occupy Indigenous people's lands.[18] Today, mining, oil and gas, and pipelines are crucial to the Canadian economy and crucial to its status as a prosperous G8 Nation in an age when much of its manufacturing base has been offshored.[19] The environmental impacts are severe. While Canadian civil society, including social justice and environmental non-governmental and activist organizations have protested politely, it has been Indigenous nations and activists who have established blockades, made meaningful legal challenges (thanks to the special provisions for Indigenous rights in the nation's 1982 constitution) and disrupted business as usual, powerfully when mines, or the railways, roads or pipelines that serve them, cut through Indigenous lands.[20] For this reason, Indigenous activists have been targeted for surveillance, harassment, and repression by the nation's police forces, often working hand-in-glove with the private security and intelligence wings or subcontractors of major mining and logistics corporations.[21]

As a result, many Indigenous intellectuals and activists have rightly identified the extractive and logistics industries, on which Canada depends, as the face of twenty-first-century colonialism.

This, in spite of the fact that the nation-state has committed itself to an official policy of 'reconciliation' with Indigenous people.[22] Extractive and logistics companies almost all have jumped on the reconciliation bandwagon, and (with government encouragement) are eager to negotiate with Indigenous people and even cut Indigenous communities in on a share of the profits from their enterprises.[23] Yet a growing number of Indigenous nations are sounding the alarm that, while such a windfall can represent an important input of cash and jobs for systematically impoverished communities, they come at a terrible cost.[24] The ecological disruption and pollution many such projects bring or threaten (for instance in pipeline or tailings pond ruptures) risk making traditional Indigenous land-based practices impossible, including hunting, fishing, and the harvesting of traditional medicines.[25] Large extractive and infrastructure projects may indeed bring money and jobs, but in often remote communities they also bring problems including drugs, the inflation of costs, reliance on outside wealth, and 'man camps': temporary housing for (mostly non-Indigenous) workers (almost exclusively men) who come to work on such projects and bring with them a market for drugs, alcohol, and sex work. Numerous studies show that the presence of such extractive and infrastructure projects is often directly related to elevated rates of gender-based violence and the national epidemic of Murdered and Missing Indigenous Women and Girls.[26]

Yet the vast majority of Canadians, who live in the nations' long-colonized cities or in rural areas never see this reality except for the occasional spectacle of an Indigenous-led pipeline blockade or land occupation when it makes headlines, and most Canadians have little or no interest in or knowledge of the extractive and logistics industries. Yet all are invested, literally and figuratively, in this twenty-first-century colonialism, which occurs not only in Canada but around the world. Some 40 per cent of capital for the global extractive corporations is raised on Toronto's Bay Street (like Wall Street, the one thoroughfare is a synecdoche for the larger financial district) and here are also the headquarters of Canada's 'big five' banks, in which practically all Canadians (and Canadian institutions) have their savings, through which they manage their investments or where their debts are brokered.[27]

Finance and Multicultural Capitalism
So, Belmore's choice of location at the headquarters of Canada's

largest bank is by no means coincidental. As I have elaborated elsewhere, the theft of lands from Indigenous people, and the elimination of Indigenous presence on those lands, has always been a financialized affair.[28] All three key dimensions of the so-called FIRE sector (finance, insurance and real estate) were essentially born in the crucible of European imperialism and (settler) colonialism: both stock markets and the joint-stock, limited liability corporation had their origins in Amsterdam and London in the financing of colonial ventures, settler colonies, and the slave trade.[29] In Belmore's few public comments about *Gone Indian* she has stressed that, in transporting a pow-wow into the financial district, she is attempting to create a spectacle not so much of remembrance of the past but a haunting image for the attendees, the vast majority of whom are urban settlers.[30] Before this space was a financialized, colonized place (the headquarters of Canada's largest bank) it was something, or somewhere, else, an Indigenous space. But the performance Belmore choreographed does not afford the viewer the satisfaction of the anthropological gaze so germane to settler colonies where, as Patrick Wolfe notes, the state attempts to continue its genocidal elimination of Indigenous presence on the land precisely by adopting, accommodating, and appropriating its chosen versions of Indigenous 'culture'.[31] 'We', the audience, arrive expecting to be entertained; we leave haunted by ghosts that were always already hidden in plain sight.

The choice of the RBC headquarters is quite specific. As Canada's largest bank not only does it inherit the legacies of financialized settler colonialism, which for instance financed the fur trade on which the nation was built, or the expansion of the railway across the nation, which led to the mass displacement of multiple Indigenous peoples. RBC is also a key participant in the continued colonization of the land today: the bulk of the savings and investments it manages are routed through firms on Canada's nearby TSX stock exchange, where by some estimates 60 per cent of global extractive industry venture financing is generated.[32] Indeed, Canada has repeatedly named the extractive industry, both at home and abroad, as one of its key strategic economic interests.[33] This in spite of the fact that numerous international non-governmental organizations, including Human Rights Watch, Amnesty International, and the United Nations have condemned Canadian and Canadian-funded mining corporations for environmental and human rights abuses both within Canada and around the world, especially as they have affected (and, indeed, targeted) Indigenous people and Indigenous lands.[34]

It is notable that, in 2009, Nuit Blanche's breakthrough year as a signature public arts event, the one-night festival sold its naming rights to RBC rival Scotiabank, an institution that, as Peter James Hudson has demonstrated with finesse, has been pivotal to the 'financial colonization' of the Caribbean, long seen by Canadian banks and their international counterparts as a Bay Street zone of influence.[35] The selection of Belmore as one of the headline acts for this iteration of the festival represented an act of constrained subversion by the curators of the Bay Street component of the festival, the Toronto collective DisplayCult. The festival occurred almost exactly one year after the great financial meltdown of fall 2008, in which Toronto's Big Five banks played a significant role and during which they quietly received a massive $114 billion (CAD) 'injection of liquidity' and loan guarantees (read: bailout) from the Canadian government.[36]

Scotiabank's sponsorship of Nuit Blanche, and other similar banks' sponsorship of similar blue-chip and populist cultural events represents an important example of the way Canada's leading capitalist firms 'buy into' and support hegemonic notions of Canadian multiculturalism in ways that reinforce what might be called a capitalist state ideology of ambiguity.[37] As with their high-profile (and much protested) sponsorship of Toronto and other Canadian cities' LGBTQ2 Pride Parades, Canadian banks are eager to associate their brand with a vision of Canada as a functional multicultural mosaic where diversity is synonymous with economic competitiveness on the world stage.[38] Here, a defanged ambiguity is the dominant aesthetic paradigm, not so much because it is the key content of all the artistic work, but because it is the syntax between them.

Underneath the multicultural superstructure that such festivities represent is the monocultural base of neoliberal capitalism with an extractivist flavour, a monoculture evident to even a casual observed who might have visited Bay Street only hours before Nuit Blanche in 2009: bustling, besuited businesspeople, who trace their heritage to all four corners of the globe (including, among them, Indigenous people), participating in the financial clockwork of Canada's economic headquarters. Though it must be noted that the upper echelons of Canadian finance remains an 'old (white) boys club', with pivotal members from Canada's long-standing political and economic 'establishment', its 'front office' appearance, and general tendency, is towards a logic of multicultural inclusion that would like to pride itself on reflecting Toronto's broader reputation as the world's most 'diverse' city.[39]

Still, this diversity is only skin deep. As Wall Street ethnographer Karen Ho notes, while investment banks may remain deeply racist institutions, they also tend to pride themselves on a certain corporate multiculturalism that resonates with a hyper-capitalist ethos and aesthetic: obeying only the ruthless logic of supply and demand, and valuing only talent and hard work, the diverse face of the firm reflects the beneficent power of colour-blind markets to help humanity transcend its regrettable mistakes of the past.[40] The preferred narrative, both within these firms and in the wider capitalist economy they (and their Canadian financial counterparts) superintend and discipline, is that now, at the proverbial end of history, there is a strict division between private multicultural expression and public corporate monoculture. Indeed, the freedoms of the former are only secured by the vitality of the latter: dress and act however you want on your own time, but here at the bank we have the corporate dress code and, more importantly, professional expectations that transcend difference.

This corporate multiculturalism is reflected by, and co-enables, the kind of shallow multiculturalism that is, in a strange way, the monocultural imperative of the capitalist settler colonial state of Canada: the economic vitality produced by an agreement on liberal democratic and neoliberal norms is the guarantee of the peace and freedom whereby each citizen might enjoy and reproduce their particular monoculture free of government interference.[41] Let us set aside for a moment the many, many occasions, past and present, when the Canadian government has intervened in the private rights of citizens to enforce white-supremacist, eurocentric or Christian (protestant-)normative values or police the allegedly 'barbaric practices' of non-normative citizens. What I want to stress is that such an approach fundamentally sequesters the category of activities labelled 'cultural' outside of the realm of politics and economics. One is free to engage in all manner of 'cultural' practices so long as they are not perceived to interfere with or challenge the reigning political and economic frameworks, only (we are told) within which (multi-)cultural freedoms are possible.

It is within this framework that dominant public and private institutions in Canada are so keen to support 'culture' as a key terrain of activity. It is precisely because 'culture' is safely separated from politics and economics that it can be so fetishized in events such as Nuit Blanche. The overarching aesthetic mood of this culture is one that dwells in and ultimately celebrates ambiguity. Belmore's provocative, radical intervention is acceptable within such a spectacle not because it itself is ambiguous and reflective of the hegemonic thrust of settler capitalism (its ambiguity is, I suggest, actively and directly hostile to that hegemony). It is, rather, that when folded into the spectacle as a whole, this, and all the many other critical and subversive interventions, appears as merely one more tile in a tolerant, open-minded, worldly mosaic. The public and private supporters of 'culture' in Canada desire and celebrate a kind of ambiguity as evidence of precisely the values and features of the successful project of multicultural settler capitalism. As long as 'culture' remains quarantined from politics and economics, its contradictions, ambiguities, and conflicts can be safely digested.

There are many problems with this approach, but for now I want to return to the particular ways in which they impinge upon Indigenous people, a friction that has much broader implications. As numerous Indigenous theorists note, for most if not all Indigenous nations there can be no clean separation between the realms of economics, politics, and culture. Anishinaabe theorist Leanne Betasamosake Simpson, for one, illuminates the deep integration of Indigenous storytelling traditions with practices of critical creative making, with modes of social and material production and reproduction, with the patterning of legal traditions and practices, and in relationship with the land itself.[42] The separation of politics, economics, and culture is, itself, a colonial notion and colonial imposition.[43] Therefore, the offer to 'include' Indigenous people in a project of state multiculturalism based on this distinction, the separation of 'culture' from a holistic and integrated way of life, is not only deeply alien, it is functionally genocidal: to accede to it would mean, conceptually and ontologically, to accept and conform to a worldview that is incompatible with Indigenous reproduction as such. On an even more material level, what would it mean for Indigenous people, who are defined as such by what Yellowknives Dene theorist Glen Coulthard calls 'grounded normativity' (a deep relational attachment to and sense of intergenerational reciprocity with ancestral lands), to be reduced to a set of 'cultural' practices detached from forms of governance (politics) and material provisioning (economics) in which that 'culture' is fundamentally embedded?[44]

Admittedly, Belmore, Simpson and Coulthard are radical voices within a diverse and often deeply divided landscape of Indigenous thought in Canada. Many (perhaps most) Indigenous people, and certainly most of the Indigenous political leadership, seek to reconcile themselves to seeking inclusion within the multicultural capitalist framework of the nation state, though with limited results given the persistence of anti-Indigenous racism and exclusion in all areas of Canadian society, from law to education, in both the public and private sector.[45] Yet the radical perspectives are the most clear-eyed, and foresee a contradiction that will continue to rear its head and lead to ever greater tensions, tensions that, if not named as the result of the contradictory logics of settler-colonial capitalism, will continue to be blamed on Indigenous people, whose 'failure to thrive' will be reduced to an unhealthy attachment to a retrograde monoculture that is unwilling or unable to adapt to the modern world.

Meanwhile, these contradictions have important implications for all people inhabiting the territories currently known as Canada. Constitutionally and economically, Canada's multiculturalism and the freedoms it affords its citizens can only exist through the ongoing genocidal elimination (or predatory inclusion) of Indigenous people, a perpetual original violence at odds with the nation state's ideological and legal claims to legitimacy, which on a material level lead, again and again, to crisis.[46] Meanwhile, such a formation inherently and implicitly insists that 'Canadians' trade the multicultural freedom to enjoy 'private' monocultural expression for acceptance of and (literal and figurative) investment in an overarching, hegemonic system of settler capitalism that, arguably, is not actually serving most people. Like most G8 nations, wages for working- and middle-class Canadians have stagnated in an age of precarious and episodic work.[47] This is to say nothing of the ongoing climate crisis that is driven by the very same logics of settler and colonial capitalism.

Bankrupt

In Canada, settler colonialism itself has taken on a financialized dimension. Since the nineteenth century, the Canadian government has imposed on Indigenous communities a form of limited 'self-governance', mandated through the Indian Act, a set of laws for the governance of Indigenous life that, at one time, included restrictions on Indigenous people's right to leave reservations without a pass authorized by a (white) Indian Agent, their right to hunt and fish, their right to practice Indigenous spirituality and ceremonies, their right to organize politically, their right to hire lawyers, their right to use modern farming implements and their right to speak their languages.[48] This Act also permitted the abduction of Indigenous children from their families to be placed in church-run Residential Schools, where they were severely punished for any behaviours deemed 'savage' (e.g. speaking their language) and where they were subject to the horrific predations and abuses of the clergy and staff. All of this is a matter of public record and discussion thanks to a landmark legal case by survivors that resulted in a national Truth and Reconciliation Commission that was ongoing during Belmore's 2009 performance and released its final landmark report in 2015.[49]

Today, the administration of settler colonialism in Canada stresses Indigenous self-governance, but the top-down colonial framework still persists: as Shiri Pasternak has demonstrated, the Canadian government exerts profound and corrosive disciplinary pressure on Indigenous governments through financialized means.[50] In the first place, the Canadian government holds the purse strings for funds that support nearly all services on Indigenous reservations and uses a series of laborious and disciplinary accounting and reporting mechanisms to constrain and delimit Indigenous communities' spending. Meanwhile, it holds out the threat of auditing and forced third-party management to dissuade those governments from taking actions that might jeopardize the colonial settler state's interests, notably blocking or intervening in attempts to locate extractive industries (e.g. mines) or infrastructure (e.g. pipelines) on Indigenous lands.[51]

Meanwhile, the same neoliberal governments have sought to fix the 'Indian Problem' through financialized means. Responsibility for the endemic poverty and horrendous health and social indicators that characterize life on reserve is transferred from the Canadian government's inaction and caustic paternalism to the failure of markets in those spaces.[52] Numerous governments have sought to dissolve Indigenous collective title to lands and transform them into individual fee simple holdings, the hope being that the introduction of private property will inspire entrepreneurialism, allow Indigenous people on reservations to borrow against their holdings, relocate to take advantage of labour markets elsewhere and, ultimately, lead them to become proper capitalist subjects.[53] Needless to say, this agenda has been strenuously rejected by many Indigenous nations, who insist that their communal, non-commodified relationship to a land base is at the heart of their existence as a people. For this reason, Patrick Wolfe and others, including Glen Coulthard and Audra Simpson, have noted that such market-oriented privatization schemes are part of a long genocidal tradition of seeking to eliminate Indigenous people's autonomous land-based existence.[54] These schemes stand in stark contrast to Indigenous practices and orientations towards land-based self-sovereign resurgence that reject colonial constructs of private property.[55]

All these dimensions factor into Belmore's performance. Settler colonialism has advanced by leveraging financialized mechanisms to transform land into property by eliminating Indigenous presence. Her temporary reclaiming of the bank's space aims, in part, to reveal the imaginary and imaginative powers at work by transforming a financialized space back into an Indigenous place. It is not insignificant that Belmore here opts to work with pennies as well, an almost worthless unit of Canadian currency that the state ceased to mint in 2012. Copper, which originally gave the penny its unique colour and which has been a major target for ecologically destructive Canadian extractive interests for generations. Yet it has also been, since before the invasion of Turtle Island, a very important material for many Indigenous cultures, used for a wide variety of cultural, spiritual, and economic purposes.[56] The toxins released by the industrialized mining, transportation, and refining of copper (as well as zinc, from which pennies were most recently made) have disproportionately affected Indigenous people due to centuries of environmental racism.[57]

Belmore's attempts to crush or pulverize this ubiquitous fetish object, stands in, perhaps, for Indigenous attempts to grapple with the poisonous financialized spirituality or belief system of settler colonialism, which in the end is reducible only to the pathological logic of capital itself: accumulation at all costs.

Belmore's failure to crush the coins, and Greyeyes' ambivalent, fractured dance, may be read as resonant with the way financialized settler colonialism, past and present, has sought to subsume or subscribe Indigenous people in a system that perpetually thwarts their thriving. As Paula Chakravartty and Denise Ferreira da Silva illustrate, the contemporary global financial order is not only built on legacies of racism and colonialism, but, because of that, creates racialized financial subjects doomed to a kind of perpetual failure that is nonetheless profitable for others.[58] In their reading, this financialized system places non-white people in a state of recurring, unpayable debt, a debt incurred as a subject who was never intended to thrive or succeed within a white-supremacist economic system, even (especially) if that system now (self-servingly) declares itself a colour-blind capitalist meritocracy.[59] The latest iteration of this is a form of what Jackie Wang and Keeanga-Yamahtta Taylor—writing about the anti-Black racism and oppression in the US leading to, during and after the 2008 financial meltdown—identify as 'predatory' financial inclusion.[60]

Belmore and Greyeyes attempt to innovate Indigenous practices within a field of coins, in the shadow of the bank, surrounded by settler onlookers; their inability to succeed or thrive then becomes evidence of an unspoken and unspeakable debt that settler colonialism imposes on Indigenous peoples and communities. As with the case of settler colonial schemes to 'civilize' Indigenous people through the financialization of their lands, the gift is poisoned.[61] It follows on the heels of how European colonists used the 'gift' of Christian religion to destroy Indigenous cultural, political, and spiritual resistance, and autonomy, the weaponized 'gift' of blankets contaminated with smallpox as a means of biological warfare, or the way in which the Canadian government stripped Indigenous people of their rights over generations through the 'gift' of enfranchisement (assimilation as Canadian citizens).[62] 'Financial inclusion' here appears as the latest mystification of what could more fruitfully be seen as a multigenerational settler colonial campaign of revenge for the ontological crime of continuing to survive and occupy sought-after land.

Yet at the same time this performance might also be said to seek to awaken the audience's sensibility to the unpayable debts owed by settler colonialism itself. With 13.5 million accounts in a nation of 36 million, it is highly probable that the plurality of spectators at Belmore's performance were invested in RBC. In this regard, all of Canada's five hegemonic banks are equivalent: settler colonial capitalist citizenship requires one be invested, one way or another, in both the symbolic and the real perpetuation of the financialized seizure and destruction of Indigenous lands via one's savings, investments, pensions, and other financial activity.[63] Further, the enjoyment of the built environment and of the rights of citizenship anywhere in Canada, and certainly in its financial capital Toronto, depends on a long history and legacy of financialized seizure of land and elimination of Indigenous presence.[64] Hence both the site of RBC Plaza and the material of the coins might be intended to awaken an awareness in the audience that they, too, are *the product and the reproducers of* a financialized form of settler colonialism, and that this system implies an almost sublimely huge moral and also economic debt.

For instance, the reparation settlement for the survivors of the Residential Schools alone (the largest for a class action suit in Canadian history, with upwards of 34,000 claimants) amounted to over $3 billion;[65] the monetary compensation and restitution for *all* historical harms, attempted genocide, and the systematic theft of Indigenous land, were it to be seriously entertained (it is not), would quite probably amount to a sum sufficient to bankrupt this G8 Nation.

Debt and Ghosts

Along with my colleagues Clea Bourne, Paul Gilbert and Johnna Montgomerie, I am exploring the usefulness of the metaphor and method of the spectral and ghostly as a means to trace the legacies and continuities of colonial violence in the contemporary financial system.[66] Such legacies can, in conservative political-economic terms, be difficult to parse, though recent efforts in the UK to account today for the residual wealth of the transatlantic slave trade, or the colonial exploitation of the Indian subcontinent are very promising, as are those in the US and Caribbean to account for the origins of today's wealth in the institutions of chattel slavery, the better to claim reparations by the descendants of those system's survivors.[67] Yet such accounting efforts quickly run into problems. In general, tracing money flows over centuries is akin to following the passage of water in the ocean's currents: it's not only that money is highly fungible but that not all transactions are recorded. Even if they were, the sources of the original funds are difficult to track. More generally still, such forensic accounting misses the forest for the trees: the money generated by world-historic acts of colonial and imperial cruelty and theft is itself only a paltry reflection of that crime, whose implications are far more profound. How does one account, for instance, not only for the wealth extracted from the Indigenous territories of what is currently called Canada when it only became 'money' when it reached the imperial metropole and was exchanged for other (also largely ill gotten) commodities? How does one account not only for the theft of Indigenous wealth but for the wholesale *econocide* of a complex network of pre-colonial systems of material provisioning that did not use money or value the personal accumulation of material wealth? Like attempts to explain Indigenous cosmologies in European languages, there is much lost in translation, and the loss is far from innocent.

For this reason, attending to the ambiguous power of ghosts is important for thinking through the ambiguous intersections of colonial violence and finance. As Mark Fisher notes, accounting for ghosts, applying what Derrida identified as a 'hauntological' method, is an attempt to contend with the 'agency of the virtual'.[68] 'The late capitalist world', he writes, 'governed by the abstractions of finance, is very clearly a world in which virtualities are effective.' Likewise, Ann Stoler notes that the study of empire is a matter of ghostly work, excavating the undeniable but at times ineffable legacies, continuities, and resonances of colonial violence and extraction through to the present.[69] Ian Baucom's *Spectres of the Atlantic* makes a strong case not only for accounting for the *quantitative* influence of the transatlantic slave trade on the ledgers of Europe, but also the *qualitative* ways in which that horrific business came to shape the methods and means of accounting for finance and its power.[70] In other words, Baucom and others invite us to consider how these exercises of colonial and racial power fundamentally reshaped the operations of financial institutions and protocols in ways that, while obscured, persist into the present day. This persistence, this haunting, finds its expression in the racist and neo-colonial ramifications of contemporary financialization, the way, for instance, the 2008 financial crisis disproportionately affected and targeted Black and Latinx Americans, the way the transnational politics of financialized debt continue to enable banks in the Global North to pillage nations in the Global South, or the predatory forms of 'financial inclusion' that seek to remedy the inequalities that stem from the legacy of colonialism with new forms of financialized exploitation.[71]

As Richard Gilman-Opalsky notes, while the powerful, the victors of history, may be keen to expel or exorcise such spectres, there is a radical politics to 'becoming ghost', to recognizing and taking up the call of the ghost for justice and the righting of historical wrongs.[72] Likewise, Avery Gordon's influential theorization of 'ghostly matter', the way historical injustices of race and class live on in the present, frames haunting as a profound call to revolutionary and transformative action.[73] In a world defined by the extortionate, domineering, and punitive financial debts of (neo)-colonial capitalism, the ghost can represent a claimant on a more profound, often unquantifiable debt owed to the oppressed and exploited.

Indigenous approaches to haunting and hauntology on Turtle Island have generally agreed that such unquiet ghosts haunt colonial institutions, including financial ones, a fact vividly emblematized by the persistent images of Indigenous people on the coins, banknotes, and financial instruments (stocks, bonds) of the settler colonial nation states and corporations that are responsible for attempted genocide. Yet as Warren Cariou points out, for Indigenous peoples, ghosts are not (as they typically are in Western cosmologies) exclusively a negative or fearful revenant, come to claim a debt; many if not most Indigenous cosmologies include deeply meaningful and intimate relationships with spirits and ancestors, many of which are helpful to the living.[74] Indeed, as with many of the world's non-Western cosmologies, many Indigenous cultures offer resources for the living to consider their roles as future ghosts. It is as a future ghost that Unangax theorist Eve Tuck, writing with C. Ree, reflects on what it means to live as an indigenous subject in conditions that, statistically, are overwhelmingly likely to lead to one's premature death. In their *Glossary of Haunting*, Tuck and Ree note that

> Settler colonialism is the management of those who have been made killable, once and future ghosts—those that have been destroyed, but also those that are generated in every generation ... Settler horror, then, comes about as part of this management, of the anxiety, the looming but never arriving guilt, the impossibility of forgiveness, the inescapability of retribution. Haunting, by contrast, is the relentless remembering and reminding that will not be appeased by settler society's assurances of innocence and reconciliation. Haunting is both acute and general; individuals are haunted, but so are societies ... Haunting doesn't

hope to change people's perceptions, nor does it hope for reconciliation. Haunting lies precisely in its refusal to stop. Alien (to settlers) and generative for (ghosts), this refusal to stop is its own form of resolving. For ghosts, the haunting is the resolving, it is not what needs to be resolved ... Haunting is the cost of subjugation. It is the price paid for violence, for genocide ... Erasure and defacement concoct ghosts; I don't want to haunt you, but I will.[75]

Conclusion

Elsewhere I have mused on the political utility of settlers in Canada embracing its imminent existential, ontological, and financial bankruptcy as a methodology by which to imagine a world beyond both financialization and settler colonialism, which I think is urgently necessary.[76] For now I simply want to conclude by stressing that at stake in Belmore's summoning of the spectres of unpayable debts is the question of in what currency, or through what terms, such debts might be repaid. As Coulthard has noted, in the name of 'reconciliation' the Canadian government has made millions of dollars of new funding available in a kind of histrionic and hypocritical generosity: the money is, after all, derived ultimately from land and resources stolen from Indigenous people in the first place.[77] Indeed, even in spite of this 'generosity', multiple levels of Canadian state administration have been found guilty in court of systematically underfunding Indigenous communities and people (especially children) relative to non-Indigenous Canadians.[78] By the same token, the colonial settler state has strongly encouraged (and at times blackmailed) Indigenous governments to accept profit-sharing agreements with extractive and logistics corporations for the (ab)use of their lands, even though the environmental and social impacts are ultimately destructive to those communities.[79] For these reasons, an increasing number of Indigenous nations and communities are resisting or rejecting monetary compensation or offers and instead—insisting on their sovereign rights to control access and use of their territories, in Simpson's words 'as they have always done'. This is a grounded sovereignty (which should not be mistaken for a replica of the Westphalian European model) that they are willing to defend through civil disobedience, blockades and, even, armed resistance.[80]

If this trend continues, the settler colonial state of Canada will soon find itself unable to pay its debts for colonialism with its own minted currency: the currency itself is a key part of the system that exacts the violence that continues to incur the debt. If that is the case, amortizing that debt will need to take place by other means, through the cessation of the economic and social violence. But this is arguably ontologically impossible within the current order: the state and the form of financialized, settler colonial capitalism with which it is entangled cannot endure a terminal challenge to the intertwined legal/political/economic logics of private property and territorial state sovereignty that such a cessation would implicitly demand. Repayment of the debt would quite literally both imply and require a revolution. In this sense, this unpayable debt is an unquiet, unreconciled, and unreconcilable ghost.

It is this ghost that Belmore, I think, is summoning or inhabiting or making kin with in *Gone Indian*. The piece appropriates and détourns the trappings of the Canadian economic system, and possesses or haunts its populist spectacle of monocultural settler capitalist multiculturalism, precisely to deliver an unspeakable, unsettleable, unsettling invoice. The invoice details not simply the tallied costs of the crimes of genocidal eliminationism waged against Anishinaabe and other Indigenous people, the loot of which somehow haunts Bay Street and RBC. It is not merely an accounting for the degradation and denudation of Indigenous monocultures but, rather, the spectre of other forms of multiculturalism, stillborn or killed off by the settler capitalist monoculture. By inhabiting the quarantined terrain of 'culture' and then refusing its separation from politics and economics *Gone Indian* refuses the very epistemological and ontological separation of that field from politics and economics and calls up the spectre of other potential social orders. The piece dwells with and mobilizes ambiguities, but not in the name of reifying a settler capitalist comfort in a multicultural cultural field based on an aestheticization of ambiguity. Rather, ambiguity here stems from what Tuck and Ree identify as the (monstrously) alien 'refusal to stop' that animates the unquiet, unrepentant, and unreconcilable ghost of Indigenous presence in a landscape where it is intended to be eliminated. It is not, as would comfort the settler capitalist imagination, simply a monoculture that refuses to die. It is the ghost of relationships beyond settler capitalist multiculturalism that could have been and that might yet be.

Notes

1   Anishinaabe is an Indigenous cultural group made up of multiple different distinct and autonomous nations whose traditional territories surround the Great Lakes.

2   The term settler capitalism is a shorthand for a system that entangles the features of capitalist accumulation and settler colonial dispossession. There is a significant debate about how these two terms might best be articulated, and which (if either) ought to have primacy. For a sample of this debate, see works including: Peter Beilharz and Lloyd Cox, 'Settler Capitalism Revisited', *Thesis Eleven* 88, no. 1 (2002), pp. 112–124; Glen Coulthard, *Red Skin, White Masks: Rejecting the Colonial Politics of Recognition* (Minneapolis and London: University of Minnesota Press, 2014); Iyko Day, *Alien Capital: Asian Racialization and the Logic of Settler Colonial Capitalism* (Durham, NC and London: Duke University Press, 2016); Robert Nichols, *Theft Is Property! Dispossession and Critical Theory* (Durham, NC: Duke University Press, 2020). It should be noted that, while settler capitalism is most self-evidently the patterning of capitalist accumulation in settler colonies (like Canada, the US, Australia, etc.) is has different articulations in each of these spaces and is also an insoluble feature of global capitalism writ large.

3   Conrad Black, 'Aboriginals Deserve a Fair Deal, but Enough with Us Hating Ourselves', *National Post*, 4 August 2017, https://nationalpost.com/news/canada/conrad-black-aboriginals-deserve-a-fair-deal-but-enough-with-us-hating-ourselves.

4   Jennifer Fisher and Jim Drobnick, 'Nightsense', *Public* 23 (2012), pp. 35–63.

5   Pierre Bélanger, ed., *Extraction Empire: Undermining the Systems, States, and Scales of Canada's Global Resource Empire, 2017–1217* (Cambridge, MA: MIT Press, 2018), pp. 178–179.

6   Julie Nagam, '(Re)Mapping the Colonized Body: The Creative Interventions of Rebecca Belmore in the Cityscape', *American Indian Culture and Research Journal* 35, no. 4 (January 2011), pp. 147–166, doi.org/10.17953/aicr.35.4.4730831320225551.

7   Belmore mobilizes the offensive term 'Indian' here ironically to refer to the settler colonial image of Indigenous people. In Canada, while 'Indian' remains a residually legally operative term, the Canadian government has, over time, replaced it with 'Native', 'Aboriginal', 'First Nations', and, more recently, in response to the preference of Indigenous communities, 'Indigenous'. Meanwhile, the term 'settler' as a reference to non-Indigenous inhabitants reflects a move to decentre the normative notions of settler colonial belonging. However, this term has been critiqued for the way it erases distinctions and power relations between non-Indigenous people, for instance between the state's 'preferred' white settlers and those non-White, non-Indigenous people whose ancestors' arrival in Canada and whose belonging in Canada is not celebrated, especially Black people whose African ancestors were brought to the Americas in bondage.

8   The Cree (Néhinaw) are a large Indigenous people, made up of many distinct nations and traditions, whose traditional territories stretch from Hudson's Bay to what are today the prairie States of the US. They are closely related to the Anishinaabe people. Pow-wows are international Indigenous cultural gatherings that occur throughout Turtle Island (North America) in which traditional dance demonstrations and competitions in specific regalia are usually a key feature.

9   Sherene Razack, ed., 'When Place Becomes Race', in *Race, Space, and the Law: Unmapping a White Settler Society* (Toronto: Between the Lines, 2000), pp. 1–20.

10 Two Spirit is a term developed by Indigenous activists from multiple distinct nations and cultures to identify forms of Indigenous gender and sexual expression that fall outside the colonial heteronormative gender binary. A variety of evidence demonstrates that, prior to colonialism, various Indigenous peoples had distinct and pluralistic frameworks for practicing gender and sexual expression, and many of these traditions are still practiced, in spite of centuries of colonial religious and political efforts to make Indigenous people conform.

11 See Max Haiven, *Crises of Imagination, Crises of Power: Capitalism, Creativity and the Commons* (London and New York: Zed, 2014).

12 See Charles C. Mann, *1491: New Revelations of the Americas before Columbus* (New York: Vintage, 2006); Audra Simpson, *Mohawk Interruptus: Political Life across the Borders of Settler States* (Durham: Duke University Press, 2014).

13 See Arthur Manuel and Ronald M. Derrickson, *Unsettling Canada: A National Wake-up Call* (Toronto: Between the Lines, 2015).

14 www.afn.ca/uploads/files/factsheets/quality_of_life_final_fe.pdf.

15 Adam J. Barker, '"A Direct Act of Resurgence, a Direct Act of Sovereignty": Reflections on Idle No More, Indigenous Activism, and Canadian Settler Colonialism', *Globalizations* 12, no. 1 (2015), pp. 43–65.

16 Shiri Pasternak, *Grounded Authority: The Algonquins of Barriere Lake against the State* (Minneapolis: University of Minnesota Press, 2017); Kino-nda-niimi Collective, ed., *The Winter We Danced: Voices from the Past, the Future, and the Idle No More Movement* (Winnipeg: ARP Books, 2014).

17 Bélanger, *Extraction Empire.*

18 Deborah Cowen, *The Deadly Life of Logistics: Mapping Violence in Global Trade* (Minneapolis: University of Minnesota Press, 2014).

19 Todd Gordon and Jeffery R. Webber, *Blood of Extraction: Canadian Imperialism in Latin America* (Halifax and Winnipeg: Fernwood, 2016).

20 Henry Veltmeyer and James F. Petras, *The New Extractivism: A Post-Neoliberal Development Model or Imperialism of the Twenty-First Century?* (London: Zed Books, 2014).

21 Andrew Crosby and Jeffrey Monaghan, *Policing Indigenous Movements: Dissent and the Security State* (Halifax and Winnipeg: Fernwood Publishing, 2018).

22 Coulthard, *Red Skin, White Masks.*

23 Hannah Wyile, '"The Currency That Is Reconciliation Discourse in Canada": Contesting Neoliberal Reconciliation', *Studies in Canadian Literature/Études en Littérature Canadienne* 43, no. 2 (2018).

24 Manuel and Derrickson, *Unsettling Canada.*

25 Julian Burger, *Indigenous Peoples, Extractive Industries and Human Rights: In-Depth Analysis* (Brussels: European Parliament, 2014).

26 'Resource Extraction Projects and Violence against Indigenous Women', in *Reclaiming Power and Place: The Final Report of the National Inquiry into Missing and Murdered Indigenous Women and Girls* (Ottawa: National Inquiry into Missing and Murdered Indigenous Women and Girls, 2019), pp. 1a:584–594, www.mmiwg-ffada.ca/final-report/.

27 Alain Deneault and William Sacher, *Imperial Canada Inc.*, trans. Fred A. Reed and Robin Philpot (Vancouver: Talon, 2012).

28 Max Haiven, 'The Uses of Financial Literacy: Financialization, the Radical Imagination, and the Unpayable Debts of Settler-Colonialism', *Cultural Politics* 13, no. 3 (2017), pp. 348–369, doi.org/10.1215/17432197-4211350.

29 Clea Bourne et al., 'Colonial Debts, Imperial Insolvencies, Extractive Nostalgias', *Discover Society*, 4 September 2018, https://discoversociety.org/2018/09/04/focus-colonial-debts-imperial-insolvencies-extractive-nostalgias/.

30 Fran Schechter, 'Belmore on Bay', *NOW Magazine*, 30 September 2009, https://nowtoronto.com/art/story.cfm%3Fcontent%3D171532; see also Kathryn Yuen, 'Nuit Blanche: Illuminating the Spectacular and the Site-Specific', *Imaginations: Journal of Cross-Cultural Image Studies/Revue d'études interculturelle de l'image* 7, no. 2 (2017), pp. 154–173.

31 Patrick Wolfe, 'Settler Colonialism and the Elimination of the Native', *Journal of Genocide Research* 8, no. 4 (2006), pp. 387–409.

32 Alain Deneault and William Sacher, *Imperial Canada Inc.*, trans. Fred A. Reed and Robin Philpot (Vancouver: Talon, 2012); Todd Gordon and Jeffery R. Webber, *Blood of Extraction: Canadian Imperialism in Latin America* (Nova Scotia: Fernwood Publishing, 2016).

33 Bélanger, *Extraction Empire.*

34 James Anaya, 'The Situation of Indigenous Peoples in Canada', in *Report of the Special Rapporteur on the Rights of Indigenous Peoples*, A/HRC/27/52/Add.2, 2014, http://unsr.jamesanaya.org/country-reports/the-situation-of-indigenous-peoples-in-canada; 'Out of Sight, Out of Mind:

Gender, Indigenous Rights, and Energy Development in Northeast British Columbia, Canada' (Amnesty International, 2016), www.amnesty.ca/outofsight; Insiya Mankani, 'Canada Should Back Up Words With Action on Indigenous Rights', Human Rights Watch, 21 June 2019, www.hrw.org/news/2019/06/21/canada-should-back-words-action-indigenous-rights.

35 Peter James Hudson, *Bankers and Empire: How Wall Street Colonized the Caribbean* (Chicago: The University of Chicago Press, 2017).

36 David Macdonald, *The Big Banks' Big Secret: Estimating Government Support for Canadian Banks during the Financial Crisis* (Ottawa: Canadian Centre for Policy Alternatives, 2016), www.policyalternatives.ca/publications/reports/big-banks-big-secret.

37 Heather McLean, 'Digging into the Creative City: A Feminist Critique: Digging Into the Creative City', *Antipode* 46, no. 3 (2014), pp. 669–690.

38 Heather McLean, 'Regulating and Resisting Queer Creativity: Community-Engaged Arts Practice in the Neoliberal City', *Urban Studies* 55, no. 16 (2018), pp. 3563–3578.

39 Sunera Thobani, 'Neoliberal Multiculturalism and Western Exceptionalism: The Cultural Politics of the West', *Fudan Journal of the Humanities and Social Sciences* 11, no. 2 (2018), pp. 161–174; Hadiya Roderique, 'Black on Bay Street: Hadiya Roderique Had It All. But Still Could Not Fit In', *The Globe and Mail*, 4 November 2017, www.theglobeandmail.com/news/toronto/hadiya-roderique-black-on-bay-street/article36823806/.

40 Karen Ho, *Liquidated: An Ethnography of Wall Street* (Durham, NC and London: Duke University Press, 2009).

41 See Himani Bannerji, *The Dark Side of the Nation: Essays of Multiculturalism, Nationalism and Gender* (Toronto: Canadian Scholars Press, 2000); Richard Day, *Multiculturalism and the History of Canadian Diversity* (Toronto: University of Toronto Press, 2000).

42 Leanne Betasamosake Simpson, *As We Have Always Done: Indigenous Freedom through Radical Resistance: Indigenous Americas* (Minneapolis: University of Minnesota Press, 2017).

43 See Jessica R. Cattelino, 'From Locke to Slots: Money and the Politics of Indigeneity', *Comparative Studies in Society and History* 60, no. 2 (2018), pp. 274–307.

44 Coulthard, *Red Skin, White Masks.*

45 See, for instance, Nancy Macdonald, 'Canada's Prisons Are the "New Residential School"', *Macleans* 2 February 2016, www.macleans.ca/news/canada/canadas-prisons-are-the-new-residential-schools/.

46 See Sherene Razack, *Dying from Improvement: Inquests and Inquiries into Indigenous Deaths in Custody* (Toronto: University of Toronto Press, 2015).

47 Sheila Block, Galabuzi Grace-Edward and Ricardo Tranjan, *Canada's Colour Coded Income Inequality* (Ottawa: Canadian Centre for Policy Alternatives, 2019).

48 Robert P.C. Joseph, *21 Things You May Not Know about the Indian Act: Helping Canadians Make Reconciliation with Indigenous Peoples a Reality* (Port Coquitlam, BC: Indigenous Relations Press, 2018).

49 'Honouring the Truth, Reconciling the Future: Final Report' (Ottawa: The Truth and Reconciliation Commission of Canada, 2015), www.trc.ca/websites/trcinstitution/File/2015/Honouring_the_Truth_Reconciling_for_the_Future_July_23_2015.pdf.

50 Shiri Pasternak, 'How Capitalism Will Save Colonialism: The Privatization of Reserve Lands in Canada: How Capitalism Will Save Colonialism', *Antipode* 47, no. 1 (2015), pp. 179–196; Shiri Pasternak, 'The Fiscal Body of Sovereignty: To "Make Live" in Indian Country', *Settler Colonial Studies* 6, no. 4 (2016), pp. 317–338.

51 Manuel and Derrickson, *Unsettling Canada.*

52 Isabel Altamirano-Jiménez, *Indigenous Encounters with Neoliberalism: Place, Women, and the Environment in Canada and Mexico* (Vancouver: UBC Press, 2013); Melanie Sommerville, 'Naturalising Finance, Financialising Natives: Indigeneity, Race, and "Responsible" Agricultural Investment in Canada', *Antipode* 2018, https://doi.org/10.1111/anti.12395.

53 Thomas Flanagan, André Le Dressay and Christopher Alcantara, *Beyond the Indian Act Restoring Aboriginal Property Rights* (Montréal and Ithaca: McGill-Queen's University Press, 2010).

54 Coulthard, *Red Skin, White Masks.*

55 Leanne Betasamosake Simpson, *As We Have Always Done: Indigenous Freedom through Radical Resistance* (Minneapolis: University of Minnesota Press, 2017).

56 Kathleen L. Ehrhardt, 'Copper Working Technologies, Contexts of Use, and Social Complexity in the Eastern Woodlands of Native North America', *Journal of World Prehistory* 22, no. 3 (September 2009), p. 213.

57 Michelle Murphy, 'Alterlife and Decolonial Chemical Relations', *Cultural Anthropology* 32, no. 4 (2017), pp. 494–503.

58 Paula Chakravartty and Denise Ferreira da Silva, 'Accumulation, Dispossession, and Debt: The Racial Logic of Global Capitalism: An Introduction', *American Quarterly* 64, no. 3 (2012), pp. 361–385; Jackie Wang, *Carceral Capitalism* (Los Angeles: Semiotext(e), 2018).

59 See also Alyosha Goldstein, 'Finance and Foreclosure in the Colonial Present', *Radical History Review* 118 (2014), pp. 42–63; Wang, *Carceral Capitalism*.

60 Keeanga-Yamahtta Taylor, *Race for Profit: How Banks and the Real Estate Industry Undermined Black Homeownership* (Chapel Hill, NC: University of North Carolina Press, 2019); Wang, *Carceral Capitalism*.

61 Haiven, 'The Uses of Financial Literacy'.

62 Daniel Paul, *We Were Not the Savages: Collision between European and Native American Civilization* (Blackpoint, NS: Fernwood, 2006); Manuel and Derrickson, *Unsettling Canada*.

63 Deneault and Sacher, *Imperial Canada Inc.*; Anna Stanley, 'Aligning against Indigenous Jurisdiction: Worker Savings, Colonial Capital, and the Canada Infrastructure Bank', *Environment and Planning D: Society and Space* 37, no. 6 (December 2019), pp. 1138–1156, doi.org/10.1177/0263775819855404

64 Brenna Bhandar, 'Possession, Occupation and Registration: Recombinant Ownership in the Settler Colony', *Settler Colonial Studies* 6, no. 2 (April 2016), pp. 119–132, doi.org/10.1080/2201473X.2015.1024366.

65 Gloria Galloway, 'First Nations Leaders Want to Rethink Residential Schools Agreement', *The Globe and Mail*, 9 May 2016, www.theglobeandmail.com/news/politics/first-nations-leaders-want-to-rethink-residential-schools-agreement/article29948063/.

66 Bourne et al., 'Colonial Debts, Imperial Insolvencies, Extractive Nostalgias'.

67 Catherine Hall et al., *Legacies of British Slave-Ownership: Colonial Slavery and the Formation of Victorian Britain* (Cambridge: Cambridge University Press, 2014); Hilary Beckles, *Britain's Black Debt: Reparations for Caribbean Slavery and Native Genocide* (Kingston: University Of West Indies Press, 2013); Ta-Nehisi Coates, 'The Case for Reparations', *The Atlantic*, June 2014, www.theatlantic.com/magazine/archive/2014/06/the-case-for-reparations/361631/; Ronald P. Salzberger and Mary C. Turck, eds., *Reparations for Slavery: A Reader* (Lanham, MD: Rowman & Littlefield, 2004); Robert Aldrich, 'Apologies, Restitutions, and Compensation: Making Reparations for Colonialism', in *The Oxford Handbook of the Ends of Empire*, ed. Martin Thomas and Andrew Thompson (Oxford University Press, 2018), pp. 696–732.

68 Mark Fisher, *Ghosts of My Life: Writings on Depression, Hauntology and Lost Futures* (Winchester, UK: Zero books, 2014).

69 Ann Laura Stoler, 'Intimidations of Empire: Predicaments of the Tactile and Unseen', in *Haunted by Empire*, ed. Ann Laura Stoler (Duke University Press, 2006), pp. 1–22.

70 Ian Baucom, *Specters of the Atlantic: Finance Capital, Slavery, and Philosophy of History* (Durham, NC: Duke University Press, 2005).

71 Zenia Kish and Justin Leroy, 'Bonded Life: Technologies of Racial Finance from Slave Insurance to Philanthrocapital', *Cultural Studies* 29, nos. 5–6 (2015), pp. 630–651; Nick Bernards, 'The Poverty of Fintech? Psychometrics, Credit Infrastructures, and the Limits of Financialization', *Review of International Political Economy* 26, no. 5 (2019), pp. 815–838; Philip Mader, 'Contesting Financial Inclusion', *Development and Change* 49, no. 2 (2018), pp. 461–483.

72 Richard Gilman-Opalsky, *Specters of Revolt: On the Intellect of Insurrection and Philosophy from Below* (London: Repeater books, 2016).

73 Avery F. Gordon, *Ghostly Matters:*

Haunting and the Sociological Imagination New edition (Minneapolis and London: University of Minnesota Press, 2008).

74   Warren Cariou, 'Haunted Prairie: Aboriginal "Ghosts" and the Spectres of Settlement', *University of Toronto Quarterly* 75, no. 2 (2006), pp. 727–734.

75   Eve Tuck and C. Ree, 'A Glossary of Haunting', in *Handbook of Autoethnography*, ed. Stacy Holman Jones, Tony E. Adams and Carolyn Ellis (London and New York: Routledge, 2013), pp. 642–643.

76   Haiven, 'The Uses of Financial Literacy'.

77   Coulthard, *Red Skin, White Masks.*

78   Marc-André Cossette, 'Fix First Nations Child Welfare System Now, Says Cindy Blackstock', CBC, 2 December 2017, www.cbc.ca/news/ politics/blackstock-philpott-children- welfare-1.4420658.

79   Shiri Pasternak, *Grounded Authority: The Algonquins of Barriere Lake against the State* (Minneapolis: University of Minnesota Press, 2017).

80   Adam J. Barker, '"A Direct Act of Resurgence, a Direct Act of Sovereignty": Reflections on Idle No More, Indigenous Activism, and Canadian Settler Colonialism', *Globalizations* 12, no. 1 (January 2015), pp. 43–65; Joanne Barker, ed., *Critically Sovereign: Indigenous Gender, Sexuality, and Feminist Studies* (Durham: Duke University Press, 2017); Leanne Betasamosake Simpson, *As We Have Always Done: Indigenous Freedom through Radical Resistance* (Minneapolis: University of Minnesota Press, 2017).

Personal Matters and Public Affairs

Hedwig Houben

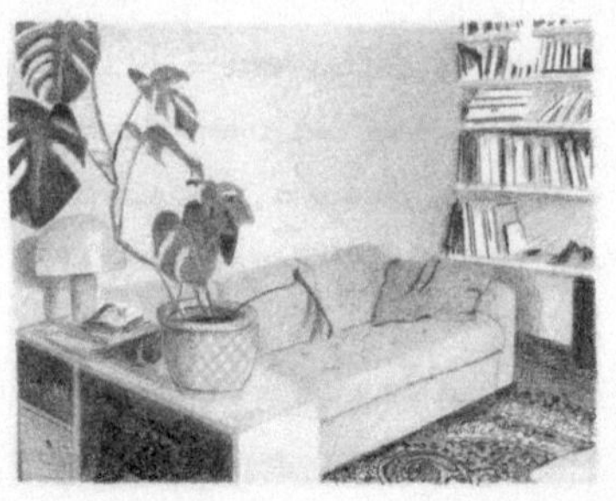

I would like to begin this talk with an introduction of two objects, which are a portrait and a car. The portrait — made out of clay — is an imitation of my face. She shows me, I'm Hedwig Houben, she is a portrait. I will call the portrait 'I' during my talk, which means that the word I can both be perceived as a pronoun and a name, a person and an object. Something which can get a little confusing along the way. It is possible that you recognize I, as she has appeared in earlier works already. She was shown in Personal Matters and Matters of Fact 2011, The Collector and Its Host and Imitator Being Made, both 2015. The other object, a car, is a new character that hasn't been part of the conversation so far. He is not made by me but modeled by others.

The car is made of grey-greenish modeling clay: plasticine. The kind that won't dry when exposed to air. From now on I will call the car 'The Other', meaning that he will represent everything that is not familiar to I. He can be a stranger walking on the street, a bright new technical device, a contemporary artwork, an exotic fruit or any other imaginable thing that is 'different'. So The Other stands for an awful lot of things. And because of this broad meaning, it's hard to come up with one clear definition of who The Other precisely is. In theory he is impossible to frame. In contrast to him, I does not have many faces. As an individual she has the quality of being separated from others and possessing her own needs and/or goals. She has her own face, her own voice, her own character and, as a matter of course, the world revolves around her. I is what novelists would call a 'flat character'. Flat characters are two-dimensional, in that they are relatively uncomplicated, and easy to read. With the result that when the reader is introduced to I, he or she can kind of guess what to expect from her. The Other, on the other hand, is referred to as a 'round character', which by contrast is a complex figure with many different characteristics, making him harder to grasp. He has no clear face, no clear voice and no clear character.

The Space where The Other is usually located is the public space. A large comprehensive field that means, in the broadest sense of the term, the space that is not private. Within this public domain, confrontation can take place between I and The Other. Meaning that as soon as I leaves the private sphere she can encouter The Other. For instance during grocery shopping, while waiting for her train, when she is stuck in traffic, etc. In fact The Other is a stranger, and I has no idea how to get an accurate impression of him. Based on his driving style she can judge him to be friendly or an asshole. But bad drivers can be great musicians and great drivers bad politicians. Hence, I needs to have some tools to navigate the uncertainties that The Other presents. Leaving home would otherwise be too stressful, as I - naturally - doesn't like to be confronted with difficulties. No thanks, please, leave me alone.

A strategy that I uses to form an opinion of The Other is the method of categorization. In which ideas, objects, people and animals are recognized, differentiaded and understood by classification. This artificial construct leads to categories on the basis of a concept. For example, animals with wings, men with red hair or people who drive BMWs. An important, almost inevitable, consequence of this method is the creation of stereotypes, where one property is isolated from a set of properties and proposed as a representative of the whole collection. I, for instance, believes that people who drive BMWs are agressive men who think they're awesome drivers. A stereotype often arises from the need to simplify the complex reality so that I can walk down the street with more comfort. But classifying can be tricky and evoke some trouble. In the end it often leads to uneasiness. Because, who decides on the categories? And what if The Other is catagorized in a group he is not happy with? What if he feels discriminated against and insulted, thinking he should belong to another group or in principle is against the formation of groups? In addition, there are others who look up to a particular group very much and would do anything to become one of them. Mostly by customizing their appearance and behavior. These 'others' are usually called imitators. Imitation is often a consequence of excessive admiration or uncertainty about themselves. One wants to be part of a group in order to feel more appreciated, less alone, stand out less or some other reason. The activity of aping in most cases is harmless, despite the fact that it hinders the classification process. I has to be extra careful in forming an opinion of what she sees. Trendsetter or trendfollower, authentic or attitude, Mercedes or Lexus.

In order to know how I should position herself in relation to The Other, she should first figure out who she is herself. Who am I? A helpful way to do so is with a change of enviroment (different circumstances), for example in situations where I moves (other neighbors). Another effective way is by heading out: I goes traveling, I becomes a tourist. Carrying a suitcase packed with only bare essentials, I is ready to have fun, pleasure, profit, an experience she will never forget. Riding a camel in Merzouga, camping on a farm in Twello, tasting wine in Saint-Emilion. All activities that can contribute to the discovery of herself should be eagerly embraced. I is even willing to drive to the other side of the world to catch a glimpse of this otherness. Other weather, other nature, other food, other habits, other languages.

But once back home I has to face reality again. "Tumble out of bed and stumble to the kitchen. Pour myself a cup of ambition and yawn and strech and try to come to life..." Meanwhile, I did learn to know herself better. What she likes, what she is good at and what is not really her kind of thing. I don't need no other, she is independent. However, sometimes it can be very enjoyable to belong to a group. In the case of taking part in a certain tradition for instance, which has a unifying effect. A yearly family trip, Christmas or Carnaval where - while loudly singing, "There is a horse in the hall..."- I puts her hands on The Others shoulders. That special 'we' feeling.

Hedwig Houben

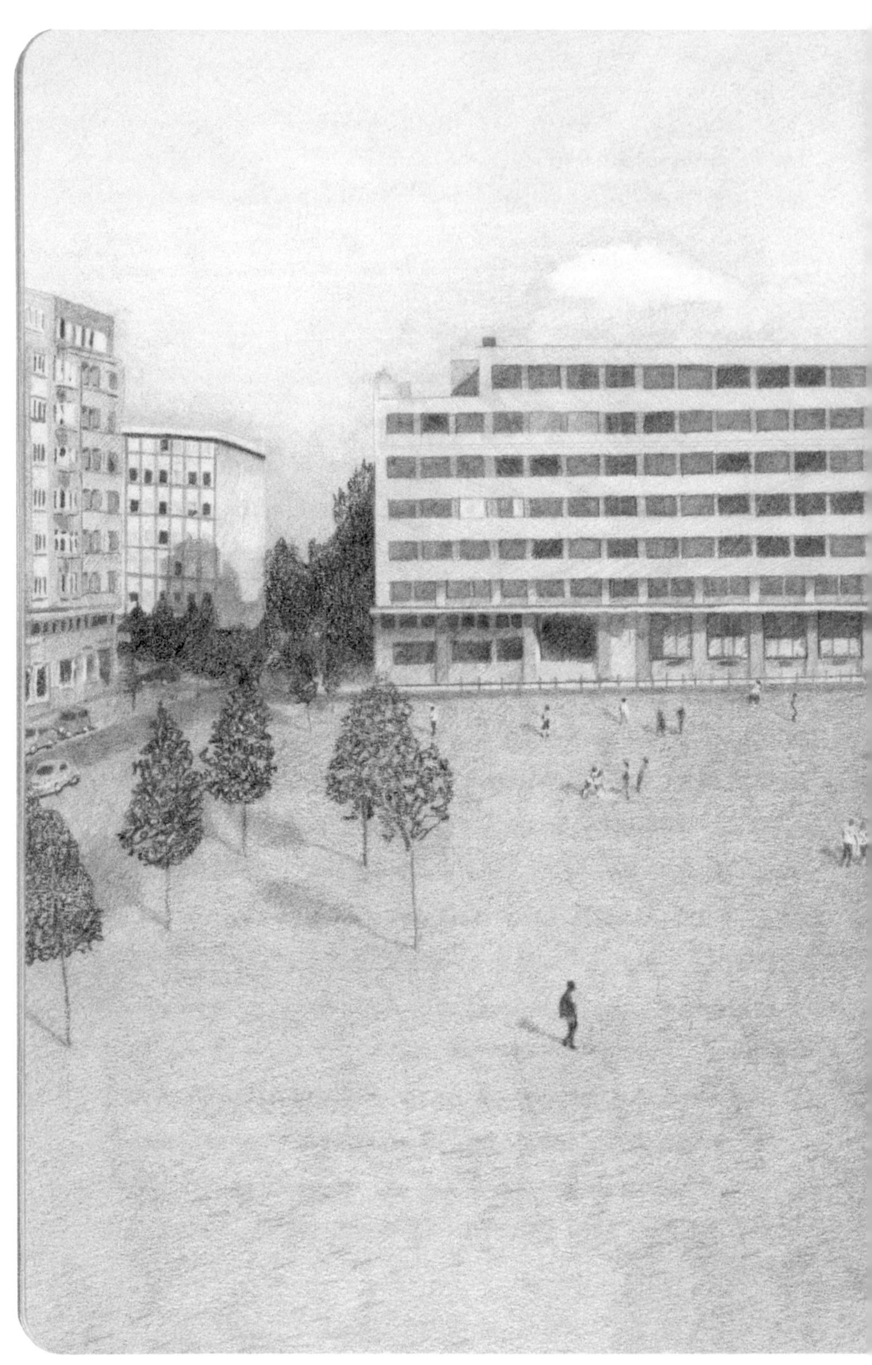

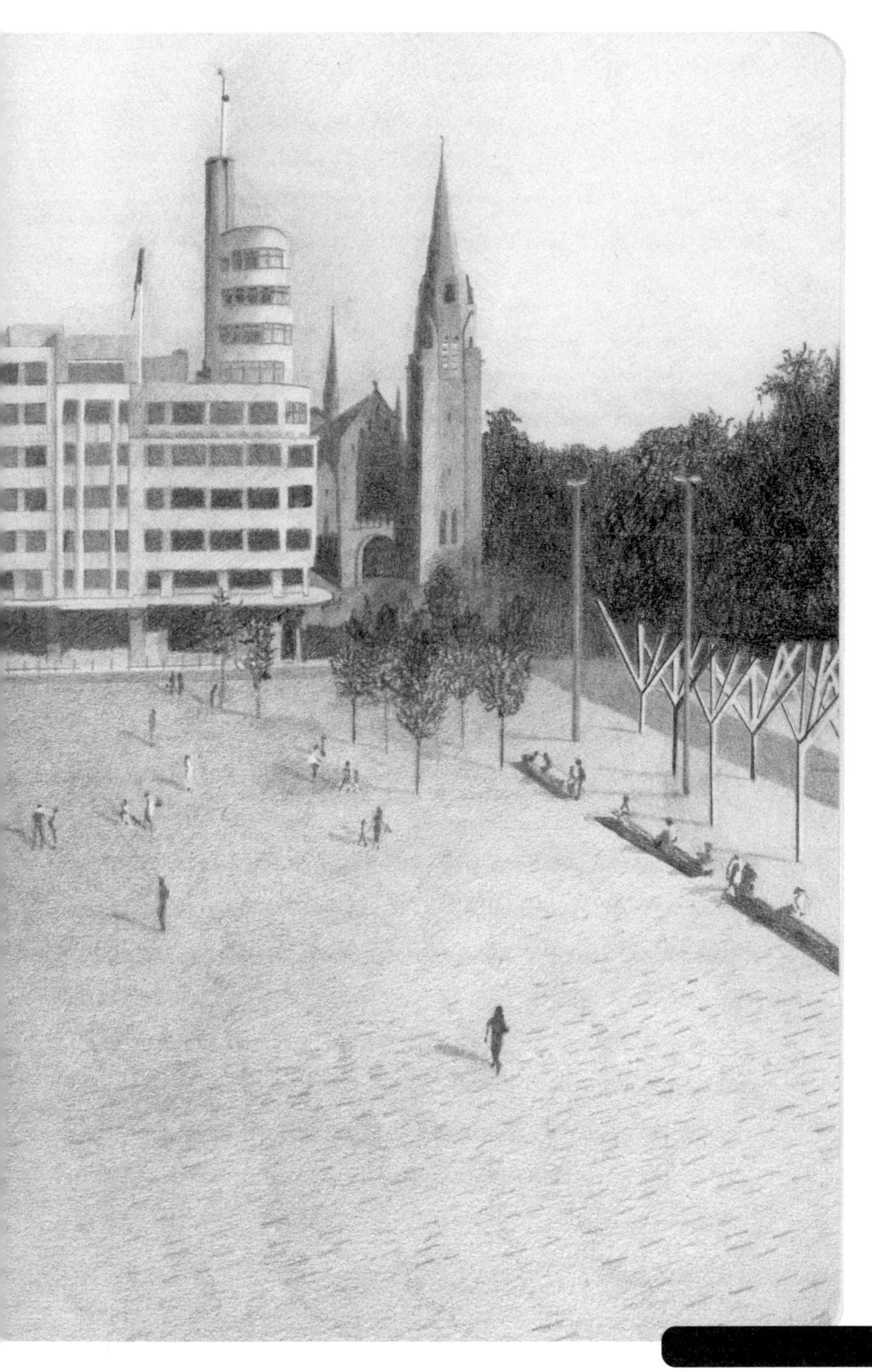

Hedwig Houben

While it is commonly assumed that traditions have an ancient history, many traditions are newer than you would expect. Often invented on purpose – whether that be out of political, cultural or commercial interest – in order to promote a group identity. That special 'we' feeling. Only 'we' is not a static concept and is always accompanied by the notion of The Other: 'you and I', 'another and I', 'others and I', or 'you, another (or others) and I'. Speaking of 'we' therefore automatically means the exclusion of others, as 'they', 'their' and 'them' are not included. Why 'they' are not part of 'us' may be for various reasons. It may arise from a slight difference in preference, in the case of a particular football club for instance. However, greater differences can also occur, when 'they' vote for a different political party than 'us', or when 'we' are less fortunate than 'them'. To ensure that these differences do not lead to an escalation, 'we' expect The Other to treat us with 'respect' and vice versa.

At the core, respect is a feeling that is revealed to The Other. It's an invisible transfer that shows that one person accepts another as a worthy and valuable human being, or a material thing. But since respect involves feelings, it's hard to control the transfer completely. It's not unimaginable therefore that I can get caught up in an inner conflict between what she feels and what she is socially expected to feel. An initial intended sense of respect can come out in the form of tolerance, acceptance or irritation, with the result that both The Other and I are left in confusion. This confusion has only grown, since at the beginning of the 21st century the word 'respect' made an entrance in youth culture and – under the influence of excessive use by rappers – has been given a subtly different meaning. "You better respect my mind cause I'll kill you", according to Z-Ro, in his song 'Respect my mind'.

Besides the usual codes of conduct that 'we' communicate back and forth with The Other, certain behavior is also expected within the group itself. Social rules tell I what is 'normal' behavior, defined by

the members of the group. Any behavior that deviates from or neglects
these rules is — in most cases — not accepted and, in a worse case scenario,
can lead to the exclusion of I. I is kicked out, no mercy.

Another thing that can lead to a break-up or fragmentation within a
group is the concept of time. Because what was acceptable in the past
may no longer be the case today. Old meets new, forwards, backwards,
modernity. Or retro: a phenomenon that has become increasingly popular
especially during the last decade. Some examples are, the Volkswagen
Beetle, the platform shoe or the bright new residential areas which
have arisen and remind one of the old days. Yesterday's design with
today's technology, the retro style is hot!
It's said that people and movements who appreciate innovation and
originality generally dislike this type of design as they see it as a form
of deterioration. Retro repeats things we already know, and therefore
it is not original, not surprising.

Raised eyebrows, wrinkled forhead, open eyelids, wide open mouth. A
surprise is ussually experienced when an expectation turns out
differently in reality. For instance, I had assumed that all men who drive
BMWs were not her type, until she fell in love. On the other hand,
others see retro design as a way to say that I is not happy with
contemporary life, as retro evokes nostalgia. In this case, retro could be
seen as a form of protest. However, dissatisfying, surprising or not,
retro style is super hot.

I likes her car. Nothing feels better than to step in her car and drive
wherever she likes. Home, work, holiday, it's all reachable because the
car fulfills her needs. Adjusting her drivers seat to a comfortable
position, making sure she has a good view of the road, playing her
favorite music loudly on the speakers. Independent, autonomous,
ready, there she goes. But I is not the only one who likes her car.
Over time, more and more cars have appeared, as The Other has

also recognized the benefits of this freedom. Adjusting his driver's seat to the right angle, making sure he has a good view of the road, playing his favorite music loudly on the speakers. Independent, autonomous, ready, there he goes. Till both The Other and I get stuck in traffic and find out that freedom also has its limitations. 'Come on, drive.' 'Not so slow.' 'You ... Damn it.' Overtaken by a feeling of helplessness, I realizes she would better stay calm and count to ten. I knows she has power, yet she is powerless. In control, out of hand. Staying at home or going out. Taking the risk or better get insurance. The pros and cons. My property.

I am largely assimilated, and my parents
were not. Largely assimilated, but not
completely. But then who is? My
running joke with L was that both
our families are from the Third World.
I move and operate freely. Too freely for
some. This is how I met L though. In the
end the chance encounter was maybe even
necessary. What better way to learn life's
responsibilities than through the simple
and the hard experiences. I am very
self-conscious. L is not in the slightest.
One mode of awareness is not better than
the other, but sometimes I think life
would be much simpler if I was not
self-conscious. I have just one vice,
the common one, which is mainly as I'm
social. I have no faith — there is no
deity, no divinity, no experiences of the
transcendental kind. In my view there
is just us, everything we know, and then
I imagine plenty of mystery. I work a lot.
L works a lot, and thus we've shared
similar stresses but also great satisfaction.
I don't feel the same without L.
I wish L was here.
                    Nav Haq

Many Voices, One World

Cultural Transformations within the Non-Aligned Movement as Revised from a Contemporary Perspective

Bojana Piškur

The title on the previous page may sound anachronistic today. After all, the concept of multiculturalism has been heavily criticized in the recent past especially for its policy of cultural integration. However, *Many Voices, One World*[1] is not a promotional slogan for multiculturalism but the title of the 1980 publication also known as the MacBride Report. The report is a product of its time and it is rather political, as it clearly shows the imbalances in global communications and how the global powers interfere in any attempt to remove a 'deep and serious inequality between developed and developing countries'.[2] *Many Voices, One World* demanded 'more voice' in the field of culture, mass media, and communications; consequently, the report caused quite a controversy when it was presented. Even though it was supported by many countries, the USA and the UK condemned it as an attack on the freedom of the press.[3] 'Freedom of press' was understood by them to mean giving privilege and monopoly of the world's information to corporate interests and big media markets. Herbert Schiller already examined such 'unexamined aspects of imperialism',[4] i.e. manipulation of information and imagery in his 1971 book *Mass Communications and American Empire*. But what were the actual forerunners of the MacBride Report? Some writers say that it was made up of 'old ideas and established principles' and that the roots of its debates can be traced to the Fourth Non-Aligned Summit in Algiers in 1973. The Algiers Summit clearly saw the rise of a more 'scientific analysis of cultural imperialism and a more specific strategy to resist it',[5] which was not limited to the fields of politics and economics but also included the cultural and social fields. From then on, the question of mass communication was regularly discussed and politicized during the non-aligned conferences in Colombo (1976), Havana (1979), and New Delhi (1983) as well as during the meetings of the newly founded Intergovernmental Coordinating Council for Information. Of course, it was no coincidence that ideas on new communication flows and networks manifested themselves strongly in the global South, especially in the context of decolonization: criticism of corporate control of media flows, the right of nations to communicate, and the question of cultural dominance became some of the concerns of the Non-Aligned Movement. Additionally, as Tran Van Dinh pointed out, the information industry raised the fundamental problem, closely related to neo-colonialism on the one hand and to the new economic order on the other.[6]

But before we delve into the global information system imbalances of that era, let me briefly describe the Non-Aligned. The Non-Aligned Movement was a transnational political project, a coalition of small and middle-sized states, mostly former colonies and developing countries, from the global south or the Third World plus Yugoslavia.[7] It functioned as a social movement in the international system, a third way between the two blocs, with the aim of changing the existing global structures and create a more just, equal, and peaceful world order. However, it was not conceived at the first 1961 conference in Belgrade; its pre-history began already with the anti-colonial, anti-imperial, and social revolutions after the Second World War. Non-alignment, as it was often stated, was not a concept of confrontation, but a policy of coexistence.[8] This is important to bear in mind; one of the key problems in the world after 1945 that the non-aligned identified was the arms race.[9] Already at the Belgrade conference they formulated the 'Programme for Peace and International Cooperation', an agreement on banning all sorts of nuclear tests, which was then also sent to presidents Khrushchev and Kennedy. During the 1970s, the disarmament issue slowly disappeared from the NAM's agenda and the economic issues, mass media, and communications came to the fore instead. In the decades that followed the movement's original enthusiasm and idealism, it seems, took a more politically and economically pragmatic turn.

So, it was no coincidence that during the 1970s and 1980s a great deal of emphasis was placed on the international information system and the need to establish a new, more equal world order for information and cultural flows. There were huge imbalances between north and south, and as one of the reports stated: almost 80 per cent of the world news flow emanates from the major transnational agencies; however, these devote only 20 to 30 per cent of news coverage to the developing countries.[10] This was primarily due to the fact that a few major agencies monopolized all the worlds' information.

What was probably the most successful incorporation of ideas on democratization of communication and mass media was the establishment in 1975 of the News Agencies Pool of Non-Aligned Countries (shortly 'the Pool' or NANAP) on the initiative of the Yugoslav press agency Tanjug. In the following year already 26 members joined the Pool, among them APS Algeria, TÉLAM Argentina, ATP Chad, GHA Ghana, Samachar India,

INA Iraq, ANIM Mali, WAFA Palestine, SUNA Sudan. As the report[11] states, some 3500 news items have been disseminated through the Pool in the first year of its existence. Mladen Arnautović, who was actively involved in the Pool told me:

> Each agency provided its own interpretation of news and reports at home and globally. The intention was that the agencies free themselves from their dependence on major international agencies, in particular from the ways these big agencies interpret world events which are subsequently supplied to the press, radio, and television globally.[12]

According to its Statute, the main objectives of the Pool were: to improve and expand mutual exchange of information; 'objective information' as the basic premise of the Pool; dissemination of correct and factual information about the non-aligned countries.[13] The Pool's intention was not to create a 'supranational news agency' but to 'fill the previously existing vacuum in the international information system'.[14] The whole system functioned through the centres of re-distribution of news by agencies such as Prensa Latina, Samachar, GHA, Tanjug, AIM, MAP, INA, and so on. The reactions against the Pool were to some degree expected and came primarily from the major Western press. The main accusations were: the Pool would be controlled by member governments; in many Third World countries the press is censored; information carried to the Pool would be unreliable; the Pool would have a monopoly of information from and about the Third World.[15] However, there were also more supportive ones, as expressed, for example, by the *Le Monde* editorial:

> The Third World rightly denounces control of news by the Western world: financial, political, cultural control ... It was thus logical that decolonization would begin one day in this field ... The Western world doesn't have any lessons to give in this domain to the non-aligned countries. It has misused formal freedoms which it now demands.[16]

A monograph, the so-called Pool book,[17] was published and presented at the 7th NAM Conference in New Delhi. The book was a common project by four press agencies from four continents and its content was approved by all 26 members at the Pool's

Coordination Committee meeting in Pyongyang in 1982. Even though the Pool ceased to exist in the mid-1990s, the book is still a valuable source of information and ideas, offering examples of strategies of resistance and diversification against the hegemonic media. It is especially worth reading today in the era of (post) post-truth, reminding us that a potential for more equal and balanced information and cultural flows already existed not so long ago.

Arts and culture were also accorded particular importance in the NAM, despite the fact that they never took centre stage at summits and conferences. The 1964 report of Heads of the State participating at the 2nd Conference in Cairo considered cultural equality one of the important principles of the NAM, at the same time recognizing that many cultures were suppressed under colonial domination and that international understanding required a rehabilitation of these cultures.[18] In the Colombo resolution (1976) emphasis was placed on restitution; the members requested restitution of works of art to the countries from which they had been expropriated. Libya introduced a draft resolution in which it stressed the following: to confirm (its) paramount right to the works of art that were looted from it.[19] And at the conference in Havana (1979) Josip Broz Tito spoke of the resolute struggle for decolonization in the field of culture. The Havana declaration also emphasized cooperation among the non-aligned and developing countries, as well as: '... better cultural acquaintance; and the exchange and enrichment of national cultures for the benefit of over-all social development and progress, for full national emancipation and independence, for greater understanding among the peoples and for peace in the world.'[20] The Delhi Declaration (1983) focused more specifically on cultural heritage and its preservation, as well as on co-operation in culture between the NAM members. One of the recommendations in the declaration referred to the collaboration of the NAM members with the Gallery of Arts of the Non-Aligned Countries, established by the City Assembly of Titograd, Yugoslavia.[21]

Cultural cooperation[22] between the non-aligned countries was based on conventions on culture and programmes of cultural collaboration. Yugoslavia, for example, had signed agreements with 56 non-aligned members and observers. These exchanges were numerous, and even though comparatively little is known about them today, they were not insignificant. In addition, between the 1960s and 1980s many new biennials opened throughout the non-aligned world: Biennial of Graphic Arts in Ljubljana (already in 1955), Triennale-India in New Delhi, Coltejer Art Biennial in Colombia, International Art Biennale in Valparaíso, Chile, Asian Art Biennale in Bangladesh, Biennial of Arab Art in Baghdad, Iraq, Havana Biennial in Cuba, and others. But only one art institution was established directly under the auspices of the NAM. The before mentioned Josip Broz Tito Gallery for the Art of the Non-Aligned Countries was inaugurated in Titograd, Yugoslavia[23] in 1984, with the aim of collecting, preserving, and presenting the arts and cultures of the non-aligned and developing countries. The document was adopted at the 8th summit in Harare, Zimbabwe a couple of years later, where the gallery was to become a common institution for all of the NAM countries. The activities of the gallery were many: alongside collecting works from the NAM countries they also organized exhibitions, symposia, and residencies, and produced publications and documentary films. Works from the collection were also shown in Harare, Lusaka, Dar es Salaam, Delhi, Cairo, and elsewhere.[24] Unfortunately, their aim to create a Triennial of Art from the NAM countries was never realized owing to the wars in Yugoslavia in the 1990s. Unlike Western colonial museums of the past, the gallery in Titograd acquired 'art of the world' solely in the form of gifts and donations, while attempting to develop its own cultural networks and frameworks of knowledge and to combine this with experiences from other parts of the non-aligned world.

It is obvious that from the beginning NAM's cultural politics strongly condemned cultural imperialism[25] and encouraged cultural diversity and cultural hybridity. Western (European) cultural heritage was to be understood in terms of 'juxtaposition';[26] this heritage would be interwoven with and into the living culture of the colonized, and would not simply be repeated under new (political) circumstances. For this reason, a 'cross-national appreciation for cultural heritages' and a local-to-local approach was extremely important. Here we could well paraphrase Achille Mbembe, in that it was important not only to generate one's own cultural forms, institutions etc., but also to translate, fragment and disrupt realities and imaginaries originating elsewhere, and in the process place those forms in the service of one's own making.[27] Aimé Césaire was also quite direct in his writings on the consequences of colonialism on the cultural heritage of the colonized people. The colonial project was not only economic-military in nature, but also affected the colonized via apparatuses of knowledge, and in this way diminished the significance of their culture and cultural production.

In a similar vein, UNESCO organized many discussions on the topic of cultural diversity, especially during the 1970s. Some of those discussions were transcribed, as for example in 'Cultural rights as human rights'.[28] It is a valuable collection of different opinions and worldviews focusing on the coexistence of separate cultures, on the distinction between world and national cultures, on cultural inequalities, and so on. UNESCO also produced a number of cultural policy studies written by experts from Third World countries around the idea of developing their own cultural models. Cultural policy in the Republic of Zaire, written by Bokonga Ekanga Botombele in 1976, was probably one of the most extreme. It lengthily describes the new doctrine called 'L'authenticité', which aimed to erase all traces of Belgian colonialism in art and culture in Zaire:

> Throughout our colonial epoch, by dint of hearing about the superiority of the cultural values of the colonial ruler, the people ended up by despising their own culture and letting themselves be convinced that the colonists were superior to them in everything.[29]

But the point behind all these discussions and cultural policies was to acknowledge cultural diversity without placing art and culture on a hierarchical scale of civilization[30] and instead open up a 'conversation across differences'.

Despite the fact that NAM countries were highly culturally diverse, the newly established contacts and exchanges provided fertile ground for debates on the relationship between the globally dominant Western culture and other cultures. To name but a few, in 1985 the Gallery for the Art of the Non-Aligned Countries organized a symposium entitled 'Art and Development', where more than forty representatives from various NAM countries took part. They discussed 'strengthening cooperation, the dissemination of knowledge, mutual rapprochement and better acquaintance of art and culture of the non-aligned and developing countries'.[31] Ten years later in Jakarta, on the occasion of the exhibition *Non-Aligned Nations Contemporary Art Exhibition*, the seminar 'Unity in Diversity'[32] was organized, where the presentations and debates were very different from those in Titograd, tackling concepts such as southern perspectives in art and the South as a place of change and solidarity. The question of the contemporary art of the NAM countries (an 'alternative view on how to understand contemporary art') was discussed, and the idea of a universalist modernism and linear development in art was rejected. The seminar pointed out some important directions. For example, it emphasized that local conditions and socio-cultural backgrounds had caused modernism to take on different forms in different places,[33] as well as the idea that the contemporary art of the South was a sign of the liberation of Third World art. Among the participants at the seminar were Geeta Kapur, Mary Jane Jacob, David Elliott, T.K. Sabapathy, Jim Supangkat, Kuroda Raiji, Apinan Poshyananda.

However, the two main concepts that constantly reappeared throughout NAM's cultural politics were humanism and solidarity. NAM's humanism took as its starting point the life of the peoples and societies that had been forcibly placed on the margins of the global economic, political, and cultural system. It was the kind of humanism which Fanon constantly demanded in his writings (he ends his book *The Wretched of the Earth* thus: '... we must make a new start, develop a new way of thinking, and seek to create a new man'[34]), a humanism that 'fuelled the Third World resistance'. As for solidarity, the 1970 Lusaka resolution stated: 'World solidarity is not only a just appeal, but an overriding necessity; it is intolerable today for some to enjoy an untroubled and comfortable existence at the expense of the poverty and misfortune of others.'[35] There were different kinds of solidarities though: political solidarity within the non-aligned (in 1974 solidarity became an important concept of the new Yugoslav Constitution and in the constitution's article 281 'solidarity with the liberation movements of the world' was especially underlined), economic solidarity between the third world countries (which was stimulated by the New International Economic Order, established at the Algeria conference in 1973), and cultural solidarity. With regard to the latter, many transnational solidarity projects, such as Museo de la Solidaridad Salvador Allende, *International Art Exhibition for Palestine, Artists of the World against Apartheid* initiative, exhibition in support of the Nicaraguan people, Week of Latin America in Belgrade took place around the world. These were not just exhibitions; they were an expression of a specific historical and political moment of these peoples' struggle for decolonization and liberation in the world.

Concepts of solidarity and humanism have become obsolete over time and have basically disappeared from public discourse. It is clear that humanism as a 'possibility of human becoming' does not suffice anymore. Also, solidarity needs to be treated with caution, as conditions can be placed on solidarity, like: with whom are we solidary and how are we solidary? The question on how to revise and reactivate both concepts is one of the burning topics for today.

Looking retrospectively, the NAM networks pretty much collapsed in the late 1980s, when the global geopolitics changed significantly. The NAM still exists today but it has not provided any alternative plans for the current geopolitical and economic situation and that has probably been one of its greatest weaknesses in recent years. It has not been able to provide any plans because the structure and aspirations of its member states have changed significantly. However, quite a few authors, Samir Amin among them, look back on the NAM as a possible way of 'de-linking'[36] (to de-link means to pursue one's own policy) from current globalization, of finding another pattern of globalization, which, as he emphasizes, does not mean reverting to the old pre-colonial or colonial state but bringing new patterns of modernity to Third World countries (the question is: what kind of modernity?). He is basically advocating the kind of political, economic as well as cultural solidarity that once existed within the NAM, but in a different form of internationalism.

Even though the non-aligned ideals, ideas, and emancipatory potential have been more or less forgotten or marginalized, the legacy of the movement's 'many voices' remains. The questions are: what has actually happened with those once powerful voices? Were they neutralized, silenced or have they simply been transformed into an all-embracing globalized 'one voice'? And perhaps more importantly: how do we reclaim those voices—politically, socially and culturally?

Notes

1 See *Many Voices, One World. Towards a New, More Just, and More Efficient World Information and Communication Order* (London: Kogan Page; Unipub, New York; Paris: UNESCO, 1980). It was written by the International Commission for the Study of Communication Problems under the auspices of UNESCO.

2 See *The New World Information Order*, written by the International Commission for the study of communication problems, presented at the third session of the International Commission (UNESCO, Commission document 31), July 1978.

3 As a consequence both countries withdrew from UNESCO, only reentering it years later.

4 As quoted in Tran Van Dinh, 'Non-Alignment and Cultural Imperialism', *The Black Scholar* 8, no. 3 (December 1976), p. 41.

5 Ibid., p. 42.

6 Ibid., p. 45.

7 The movement's original principles were peaceful co-existence, respect for each other's territorial integrity and sovereignty, non-aggression, non-interference in domestic affairs, equality, and mutual benefit.

8 Josip Vrhovec, 'Tito, Non-Alignment, Contemporary Times', in *Tito-Non-Alignment-Contemporary Times* (Beograd: Memorial Center 'Josip Broz Tito', 1989), p. 18.

9 https://yuhistorija.com/int_relations_txt01.html. However, not everything was as idealistic as written in the NAM reports and documents. Many NAM countries supplied weapons and arms to other NAM countries. Historian Tvrtko Jakovina writes that Yugoslavia was not an exception and helped to arm Zimbabwe, Algeria, Guinea, Guinea Bissau, Namibia's resistance movement SWAPO, Zambia, Sri Lanka, Angola, Ethiopia, Zambia, Libya, and Egypt.

10 Christian Fuchs, 'The MacBride Report in Twenty-first-century Capitalism, the Age of Social Media and the BRICS Countries', *Javnost/The Public* 22, no. 3 (2015), pp. 226–239, doi.org/10.1080/13183222.2015.1059626.

11 Hifzi Topuz, *The New Agencies Pool of Non-Aligned Countries*, CC-77/CONF.606/COL.6, UNESCO, Colombo, 15 November 1977, p. 2.

12 Interview with Mladen Arnautović, December 2017, Belgrade.

13 Topuz, *The New Agencies Pool of Non-Aligned Countries*, pp. 2–3.

14 Ibid., p. 3.

15 Ibid., p. 6.

16 As quoted in ibid., pp. 6–7: 'Les non-alignes et l'information', *Le Monde*, 15 July 1976.

17 *News Agencies Pool of Non-Aligned Countries*, published by Indian Institute of Mass Communication, New Delhi for Coordinating Committee, 1983. English, French, Arabic and Spanish versions of the book were printed.

18 Conference of Heads of State or Government of Non-Aligned Countries, Chapter XI 'Cultural, Scientific and Educational Cooperation and Consolidation of the International and Regional Organisations Working for This Purpose', NAC-II/HEADS/5, Cairo, October 1965, p. 33.

19 At the 5th Conference in Colombo in 1976, Libya introduced a draft resolution where it introduced facts of how the country was deprived of its 'human cultural heritage' as a result of colonialism.

20 *6th Summit Conference of Heads of State or Government of Non-Aligned Countries, Havana, Cuba, from 3 to 9 September 1979, Document*, pp. 86, 87.

21 *7th Summit Conference of Heads of State or Government of Non-Aligned Countries, held at New Delhi, India, 7-12 March 1983: Document*, A/38/132, S/15675, p. 133.

22 For more on cultural exchanges see Teja Merhar, 'International Collaborations in Culture between Yugoslavia and the Countries of the Non-Aligned Movement', in *Southern Constellations: The Poetics of the Non-Aligned* (Ljubljana: Moderna galerija, 2019), pp. 43-70 (catalogue).

23 Today Podgorica, Montenegro. The collection has been part of the Contemporary Art Centre of Montenegro since 1995.

24 For more information about the collection see *Umjetni ke zbirke Centra savremene umjetnosti Crne Gore* (Podgorica: Centar savremene umetnosti Crne Gore, 2010) (introduction in English).

25 Speech by President Tito at the *6th Summit Conference of of Heads of State*

or Government of Non-Aligned Countries in Havana, Cuba in 1979, where he spoke of the 'resolute struggle for decolonization in the field of culture'.

26 See Vijay Prashad, *The Darker Nations: A People's History of the Third World* (New York and London: The New Press, 2007), p. 82.

27 See Achille Mbembe and Sarah Nuttall, 'Introduction', in Achille Mbembe and Sarah Nuttall, eds., *Johannesburg: The Elusive Metropolis* (Durham, NC: Duke University Press, 2008).

28 *Cultural rights as human rights*, Studies and documents on cultural policies 3 (published by the United Nations Educational, Scientific and Cultural Organization, Paris, 1970).

29 *Cultural Policy in the Republic of Zaire* (Studies and documents on cultural policies) (Paris: The Unesco Press, 1976), p. 52.

30 Dipesh Chakrabarty, 'Legacies of Bandung: Decolonization and the Politics of Culture', in exh.cat. *Postwar: Art Between the Pacific and the Atlantic, 1945–1965* (Munich: Haus der Kunst; Prestel, 2017).

31 Galerija umjetnosti nesvrstanih zemalja, 'Osnovna dokumentacija', Titograd, 17 December 1981, spiral bound.

32 The transcripts of some of the discussions of the seminar are accessible at: Geeta Kapur and Vivan Sundaram Archive at Asia Art Archive: https://aaa.org.hk/en/collection/search/archive/another-life-the-digitised-personal-archive-of-geeta-kapur-and-vivan-sundaram-geeta-kapur-manuscripts-of-essays-and-lectures/object/the-recent-developments-of-southern-contemporary-art-avant-garde-art-practice-in-the-emerging-context.

33 Jim Supangkat, 'Contemporary Art of the South', in *Contemporary Art of the Non-Aligned Countries: Unity in Diversity in International Art. Post-Event Catalogue* (Jakarta: Balai Pustaka, Project for the Development of Cultural Media, Directorate General for Culture, Department of Education and Culture, 1997/1998), p. 26.

34 Frantz Fanon, *The Wretched of the Earth* (New York: Grove Press, 2004), p. 239.

35 *Resolutions of the Third Conference of Non-Aligned States, Lusaka, September 1970, with Selected Conference Statements and Comments* (Johannesburg: The South African Institute of International Affairs, 1971), p. 3.

36 'Globalisation and its Alternative: An Interview with Samir Amin' (Tricontinental Institute for Social Research, notebook 001), 27 January 2019.

Cultural Cannibalism and the Subversion of Monoculture in Brazil

Christine Greiner

In the 1920s, cultural cannibalism or anthropophagy became a reference to Brazilian culture. Rituals of cannibalism have been a current practice in Amerindian and Afro-Amerindian culture since the sixteenth century. However, it was in São Paulo, after the 'Week of Modern Art' in 1922, that anthropophagy turned to be a metaphor and a way of thinking about cultural devouring strategies that characterize the eclectic appetite and mestizo ways of producing life and arts in Brazil.

Indeed, there are some possibilities of understanding cannibalism as a strategy of subversion of monocultures and, even among Brazilians and Latinos, it has been interpreted in different ways, according to the political context.

I will first give a brief historical overview to highlight some important questions that clarify what this devouring practice is all about. The purpose of this article is to think about cannibalism today as a *task still to be accomplished*, which means as an overture to multiple paths, in order to deal with *otherness as a state of creation*.[1]

In terms of methodology, this interpretation that sees anthropophagy as a task, recalls the way Jacques Derrida interpreted Marxism in his book *Spectres de Marx*.[2] According to Derrida, Marxism doesn't necessarily need to be considered as a doctrine, but could be understood as a task in the sense of some of its assumptions that still seem to reverberate, despite the radical conceptual changings of work, politics, and economy.[3]

By subverting machinic dualisms that strengthen ways of thinking that inevitably depart from the opposite notions of nature and culture, national and foreign, friend and enemy, this article assumes that anthropophagy can be understood as an epistemology of collective and cultural ambiguous bodies.

The Early Beginnings and the Oswaldian Revolution
The Week of Modern Art took place in São Paulo from 11 to 18 February 1922. Despite the ideological pressure for progress and modernity that pervaded the early 1920s, this event was not related to any commercial target or international policy. It was organized by the poet Oswald de Andrade and a group of avant-garde artists working in various artistic fields (visual arts, literature, theatre, and music).[4] The primary step was to criticize the notion of identity policy, which could be considered a critical path away from the goals of the 'Centennial Expo of Rio de Janeiro'

that happened at the same time. This Expo was primarily focused on seeking a sort of 'nationalism for export', guided by foreign models of modernity and civilization in order to assert a new image to the world of Brazil as an independent nation.[5] On the other hand, the Week of Modern Art had little impact at the time but deployed initiatives that have left key brands, such as the work of the painter Tarsila do Amaral, the *Anthropophagic Manifest* (*Manifesto Antropófago*) and *Pau-Brazil Poetry*, both written by the Oswald de Andrade, and the novel *Macunaíma,* by Mário de Andrade. In 1923, Tarsila, as she was known, travelled to Paris and studied with Fernand Léger, among others. It was during her stay in France, that she painted one of her most important works, *A Negra.* One of the subjects presented in various works such as *Morro da Favela* (1924), *Lagoa Santa* (1925), and *Abaporu* (1928) was to create Brazilian singularity with the liberty of using different techniques and gazes like the movements she experienced in Paris (Cubism, Futurism and Expressionism). Like Tarsila, Oswald and Mário de Andrade's proposal was to use the 'cannibal logic' of Indians as a metaphor to mark the Brazilian talent for devouring foreign cultures—from both outside of Brazil, such as European cultures, and from within, such as the Amerindian culture and that of African Americans—by digesting all according to their own peculiarities.

In this ambiguous cultural soup, it is possible to identify, especially in Oswald de Andrade, the remains of French Surrealism, a trace of Nietzschean proposals, and murmurs of Walt Whitman's poetry, which were important references for the writers of the Paulistana elite, who were interested in exploring different avant-garde processes of creation, outside the scope of the most conventional aesthetic models.

Always in good spirits, Andrade created a series of parodies including a translation of the Hamlet dilemma 'to be or not to be', which became 'Tupi or not Tupi'.[6] In 1929, he wrote the article 'Porque Como' (Why I eat), as an answer to the most nationalist Brazilian thinkers, and signed this text as *Marxillar,* by joking with Marxism and Jaw, because in Portuguese the word 'jaw' is translated as 'maxilar'.

Andrade considered Marx a romantic *antropófago,* and that's why he tried to read the Communist Manifesto in cannibal terms. According to him:

> The *antropófago* will inhabit Marx's city. The pre-histor-
> ical dramas ended. The means of production socialized.
> The syntheses we look forward to since Prometheus are
> founded. When the last screams of war announced by the
> atomic bomb have finished ... And because the last man
> willing to change nature will transform his own nature ...
> Nothing exists outside Devouring. The being is pure and
> eternal Devouring.[7]

In a way, the Centennial Expo and the Week of Modern Art shared the common purpose of defining Brazilian culture. However, their understanding of culture and nationalism was completely distinct. The Centennial Expo was based on settings such as territory, language, and nation; and it was focused on expectations for the international view of Brazil, by reinforcing the myth of an exuberant and exotic nation even when the main objectives were to transform the country into a modern nation. This project of increasing modernity was based on patterns established by the notions of progress, new technologies, and international markets rather than on local needs. By contrast, the Week of Modern Art in São Paulo was a preliminary attempt to create a singular and subjective strategy related to the notion of anthropophagy, and it was revived many times in different circumstances such as during the concrete movement of the 1950s, conducted by the semioticists Haroldo de Campos, Augusto de Campos and Décio Pignatari; in the neoconcretism of the 1960s, with the poets Paulo Leminski and Ferreira Gullar, the visual artists Lygia Clark, Lygia Pape, and Hélio Oiticica; and by the singers and composers Caetano Veloso and Gilberto Gil, who cannibalized foreign music (instruments and rhythms) to produce the Tropicalismo or Tropicália musical movement of the late 1960s, which was a strong political reaction to the Military Dictatorship (1964–1985).

In a broader sense, one may conclude that, despite the differences, all these artists addressed some sort of anthropophagical perspective, which involves: (1) a poetical and political attitude to deal with life by looking for zones of potential; (2) the recognition of the singularity and the diversity of experience, avoiding the tendency to transform everything in *a priori* categories; (3) the desire to enhance the perceptions of the body, without the domination of rational thoughts, by using intuition and empathy to rethink the boundaries of knowledge; (4) the denial of identity as something essential, static, or monolithic; and (5) the recognition of the self as a dynamic cartography of thoughts, feelings, and actions.

The Epistemology of the Shaman

As the anthropologist Eduardo Viveiros de Castro explained in his book *Metafísicas canibais*[8] (Cannibal Metaphysics), the roots of Brazilian culture are not European but primarily connected to Amerindian perspectivism, which means a particular form of 'multinaturalism'. As a result of this cosmology from the Amazon region, nature cannot be separated from culture. Instead of either natural or cultural productions, there are multiple perspectives. In other words, when we see something from a different perspective, it means we can deal with new realities (and not only with new interpretations of an *a priori* reality). Therefore, the anthropophagic strategy can be considered a subversive methodology to criticize the view of the colonizer by translating the imaginary stereotypes of the colonized through a multitude of ideas, feelings, and images. This point of view creates, more than a multiculturalism, a multinaturalism of bodies and experiences.

Indeed, according to Viveiros de Castro, the Tupinambá cannibalism was, since the early beginnings, a very elaborated system for the capture, execution, and ceremonial devouring of enemies.[9] The prisoners of war were usually people of the same language and customs as the captors, and they could live comfortably with them before meeting death in the central square of the village. Actually, before they were killed, the captors offered women from the village to the prisoners, so they would become brothers-in-law to their future assassins. In Tupi-Guarani language, enemy and brother-in-law are the same word *tovajar*—a term meaning 'opposite' or 'borderline'. That's why in Amerindian predation there is also some sort of affinity.

The cycle of cannibalism culminates in the execution of the prisoner. The man who kills the victim gains a new name after the act, plus the right to marry and have children, the right to speak in public, and free passage to paradise after death. The members of the community can eat the body of the deceased, except the executor, who, besides not eating the deceased, enters a period of mourning that is a kind of identification with the one who has just been executed. The aspect of sacrifice in this process is due to the revenge of the village's dead—avenged and celebrated by the execution and devouring of the prisoner.

But what is actually devoured during the ritual? The substance, flesh itself, was just a tiny piece, almost irrelevant. Therefore, it seems that the devoured 'thing' was indeed a sign meaning the enemy's relationship with the community, or in other words, his condition as an enemy. What is assimilated from the victim is the sign of *otherness*. Therefore, one may conclude that cannibalism would be a paradoxical movement to deal with execution and devouring from the enemy's point of view because the 'thing' that is devoured, is the *difference*.

Part of this process is also present in Amazonian shamanism, which represents the cross-communication between two worlds that actually cannot communicate to each other. According to Kopenawa, the shaman is a kind of *rapporteur* who goes from one point of view to another.[10] He embodies and relates the potential differences inherent to the diverging perspectives that constitute the cosmos. The power of the shaman derives from the differences between these worlds and there is also an epistemology around this ritual, which is opposed to the messianic culture because it is a primitive force of resistance to the indoctrination of the colonizer. It is not like an organized resistance, like those movements that were planned, for example, during the periods of catechization, colonialism, and military dictatorship. It is rather a carnivalesque insurrection that triggered the devouring of images, narratives, and movements in a chaotic way.

In this sense, indigenous cannibalism should always be interpreted in a symbolic instance, not restricted to the literal act of devouring the flesh. This symbolic moment of the process is called anthropophagy.

Dealing with the Colonial Discourse

An important statement of the colonial discourse is its dependence on the concept of 'fixity' in the ideological construction of *otherness*. However, as a sign of cultural and historical difference, it seems to be a paradoxical mode of representation. Homi Bhabha points out that it connotes an unchanging order as well as a disorder, at the same time.[11] Like all stereotypes, which are the main focus of the major discursive strategy of the colonizers, this ideological construction of *otherness* vacillates between what is always 'in place'—and is already known—and something that needs a representation that could be interpreted as a process of subjectification.

In this context, even if the forces of power attempt to reduce all processes to prior political normativity, there is always an articulation of differences. The main point is to avoid the notion of essential identity as observed by Edward Said in his book *Orientalism*[12] of the late 1970s, and also to recognize the dangers of a 'unique history' as noted by the Nigerian writer Chimamanda Ngozi Adichie.[13] When we try to encapsulate a complex culture in a single essence or history, we start working with stereotypes, which seems to be the primary points of subjectification from colonial discourse, for both the colonizers and the colonized.

This avoidance of fixed identities is an important starting point for contemporary Brazilian artists and intellectuals, such as the already mentioned anthropologist Viveiros de Castro; the sociologist Jean Tible, who has recovered an important bond between Marxism and Amerindian culture through a reinterpretation of the work of Peruvian journalist José Maria Mariátegui (1894–1930); and the psychoanalyst and philosopher Suely Rolnik, who has researched the evolution of anthropophagical strategies after the experiences of Lygia Clark in order to develop an original hypothesis about Brazilian colonial unconsciousness and anthropophagy as a possible strategy of insurrection.

These researchers have observed that the fracture is always deeper than we thought, and it cannot be restricted to the poetic experiences of the avant-gardes from the 1920s. Through anthropophagy it is possible to question the very notions of subject, identity, human, culture, and nature. Thinking about contemporary debates, these questions became more important than the ritual *per se*. The key is to focus on the possibilities of dislocation. For example, when Jean Tible studied the work of Mariátegui, he was not particularly interested in Peruvian history, but mostly in analyzing recent political manifestations in urban space, such as the big movements from June 2013 that happened all over Brazil.[14] Mariátegui has proposed a connection between Marxism and Indigenous America to think about the power of the collective. To make sense of what he has identified, it was important to set aside some of the references to 'Inca communism' as rhetorical flourish. He was looking for 'a culture of solidarity' that could contribute to the building of socialism in Perú. He believed that the indigenous population, descended from the Incas, gathers very favourable conditions where primitive agrarian communism survives in concrete structures and in a deep collectivist spirit. Mariátegui saw the indigenous question as providing the key to unlock the socialist revolution. He had both knowledge and appreciation of the long history of indigenous resistance: first to the Spaniards, and then to the Republic. By reading Mariátegui's research and other sources related to Brazilian cannibalism and shamanism, Tible has tried to create possible connections to better understand the emergence of collective movements through cultural singularities.

From another point of view, Suely Rolnik has thought about cannibalism and anthropophagy as a cognitive tool to deal with our colonial unconsciousness without subservience.[15] She was inspired by the Brazilian artist Lygia Clark. In her essay 'Politics of Flexible Subjectivity: The Event Work of Lygia Clark', she considered four types of producers that emerge from our past experiences: the creators, the consulting professionals (of the business and marketing world), the consumers, and the human self-presentation specialists (personal trainers, personal stylists, plastic surgeons, interior designers, and so on).[16] Among them, one can recognize those trying to create a rigid identity in order to be included in the global market, and also those operating at the micropolitical level, looking for flexible ways to deal with art and life. There are always several territories of ambivalence to 'becoming-other' with a degree of instability that comes and goes, by representing new possibilities of communication, from invisible levels of perception to explicit discourse.

Alongside the discussions conducted by these intellectuals, the Lia Rodrigues dance experience at the Favela da Maré (Maré Shantytown) in Rio de Janeiro, can also be a good example of anthropophagical strategy of creation as a contemporary task in order to nurture collective movements in a context of extreme vulnerability.

In 2003, Rodrigues moved her company Lia Rodrigues Companhia de Danças (founded in 1990) to the Maré community —which is almost a city within the city of Rio de Janeiro, with 138,000 inhabitants. Since then, she has conducted important artistic work there. The community work began with the presence of the dance company at the Casa da Cultura da Maré, which is a kind of warehouse located just beside the Centro de Estudos e Ações Solidárias da Maré (The Maré Centre of Studies and Acts of Solidarity [CEASM]), a nongovernmental organization. The building is always open so people can come in whenever they want. During the rehearsals, a few young members of the community asked to participate and were included in Rodrigues' company (Leonardo Nunes Fonseca was one of the first and continues to participate in the company today). Some of the dancers provide free workshops to the community, and several choreographers, including international artists such as the French choreographer Jérôme Bel, have presented pieces in the warehouse, thus creating a very unique environment.

Like Rolnik, Rodrigues was also inspired by Brazilian artist Lygia Clark's proposition of the 'collective body'. Clark created several performances between 1964 and 1981, focusing on the dissolution of boundaries between artists and audience. Rodrigues made a connection between Clark's work and Susan Sontag's discussion of the modern understanding of violence and atrocity in *Regarding the Pain of Others* (2004) to consider empathy in relation to the performer/audience connection and the feeling that, for a brief moment, someone can be in the place of another.[17]

Testing a collective empathic body in a shantytown like Maré is a huge challenge. How can a well-educated choreographer born into a rich white family empathize with, much less feel like, an inhabitant of Maré? Rodrigues and her dramaturge Silvia Soter are very aware of this barrier. They don't pretend there are no social differences between the artists and their audience/community. Quite to the contrary, the artistic research starts with the awareness of differences and seeks a possible exchange of singularities. Therefore, it is important to recognize a political strategy in the way she organizes her dance, and not just in the structure of her organization and its relation to the community and its location.

Aquilo de que somos feitos (That what we are made of) from 2000, was her first work inspired by Clark, who explored in greater depth the perception of the body and its relationship with objects in works like *Objetos Relacionais* (Relational Objects, created from 1976 to 1981); or the body within a group, as in *Baba Antropofágic* (Antropophagic Drool, 1973). *Baba Antropofágica* was part of Clark's body of work entitled *Arquitetura Orgânica ou Efêmera* (Organic or Ephemeral Architecture, which she began in 1969). All participants placed a spool of coloured thread in their mouth; the end of the unwound thread was in the mouth of another participant who was stretched out on the floor. This event was inspired by Clark's dream of an unknown material endlessly flowing from her mouth, material that was actually her own inner substance. *Objetos Relacionais* attempted to relate therapeutic

practice and artistic experience. These were created in the last phase of Clark's work, in which she developed a vocabulary of relational objects for emotional healing. She continued to approach art experimentally but made no attempt to establish boundaries between therapeutic practice and artistic experience, and at this point she was no longer interested in preserving her status as an artist. She started using the relational objects on the bodies of audience members/patients by stimulating connections among the senses in order to awaken the body's memories. The objects were made of simple materials such as plastic bags, stones, and sand, which acquired meaning only in their relation to the participants. The physical sensations stimulated by the relational objects as Clark used them on a patient's body, communicated primarily through touch, stimulating connections among the senses and with the body's traumatic memory.

Rodrigues did not intend to reproduce these experiences but to explore in her own way the breaking of barriers between artists and audience. By reinventing body knowledge through dancing, she creates alternative modes for a life without false utopias and illusory hopes. This is her corporeal project, which really seems to be more effective than many forms of verbal discourse, especially since the trilogy *Pororoca, Piracema and Pindorama*, which started in 2009, and was completely created at the Maré space. The last pieces, *Para que o céu não caia* (For the Sky not to Fall, 2016) and *Furia* (Furious, 2018), became even more radical in the sense of blurring the instances of life and art.

For the Sky not to Fall, for example, was completely connected to the notion of anthropophagy. It was actually based on the book *The Falling Sky*.[18] This narrative was based on the words of the shaman Davi Kopenawa, after his conversation with Bruce Albert, a French anthropologist, born in Morocco. Kopenawa speaks to be heard by those who do not understand his language. He explains it is important to listen to the forest, especially to the things that constitute the 'deep' forest. What is at stake, is not only the description of a world, or the venturing of a political activist. In this context, talking is important to defend what is left behind—the forest and its animals.

The sky will collapse if nature continues to be disrespected and the thermodynamic imbalance becomes radicalized. Kopenawa points out that white people do not seem to care about it, but the event no longer depends on them. In the forest, politics is the words of Omama (Yanomami demiurge) and the Xapiri spirits. These words can be listened to during dreams. However, the white people sleep a lot but only dream about themselves.

By contrast, the shamanic dream induced by hallucinogens is the way to know the invisible foundations of the world. It is a dream of the other. Indians and shamans are not interested in gold, merchandise, or greed, which seems like a fiction to neoliberal system of believes.

By looking for a connection with Kopenawa's words, Lia Rodrigues and her dancers dared to dream of the other, and at Maré, there are many others. The dancers have especially studied the junkies, who became examples of the shantytown's bare life. We can assume the choreography constructs an *incarnate biopolitics*, as a way of existing without exterminating what is not the same. This cultural cannibalism became the first source of resistance.

As has been widely discussed by several authors (e.g: Lemke 2011, Esposito 2008),[19] Foucault's concept of biopolitics was, after his death in 1984, received in different ways. Negri and Hardt, for example, have proposed a distinction between biopower and biopolitics. According to their books (*Empire*, 2000, and *Multitude*, 2004),[20] biopower represents the power over life and biopolitics refers to the possibility of a new ontology that derives from the body and its forces. By reading Foucault, they agreed that if there was no resistance, there would be no power relations. Resistance, and specifically body resistance, always comes first. Therefore, when I speak of 'incarnated biopolitics', I'm thinking about these forces of the body constituted by dancing. It is not the power over life, but the power of life as a creative force to deal with radical devastation.

Another good example of anthropophagical artistic experience was the project *1000 Houses*, conducted in Teresina (Piauí) by the choreographer Marcelo Evelin and the artists group Núcleo do Dirceu.[21] The proposal emerged from a concern within the Núcleo as they thought about the possibility of creating a place for spectators outside the theatre seats. The procedure was quite simple: the artists started to go into the homes of the Grande Dirceu district (where the collective was based) to generate what they called a 'co- responsibility Yf residents in art'. The interventions consisted of 'visits' or 'break-ins'; arriving without having been invited, to preserve the surprise effect. Each participant chose a

profile of homes to visit and a performance to do according to a list of criteria linked to the features of the chosen house (such as having tiles or white walls), or to the characteristics of the people living there (elderly residents), or also to an event (homes where domestic violence had occurred). Regardless of the choice, the artists' focus was always on the performativity of the encounter and the dialogue with the other, as well as on the creation of environments that were real (meeting face to face) but also fictitious (the narrative built from the dialogue with the resident). One of the intentions was to approach the private place with a public act. As the group explained on their website:

> In the actions that we developed, private became public and vice versa, in an inversion that also blurs the notion of artist and spectator and the meaning of what art sphere is established politically by sharing what is common. And the private sphere [is defined] because the event takes place in the singularity of the individual, in his or her particular universe. With predefined themes for the performances in the homes—such as domestic violence—the artists generate an interest in art in the residents while proposing a joint participation and performing a public act in a private space, which results in a deliberate blurring of the function of the actor and the spectator.[22]

Aside from the installations that presented fragments of narratives and movements created during the visits, the project was turned into a book,[23] which gathered different documents (mainly photographs) on these experiences. In this case, the anthropophagical trace of these actions is the devouring of *otherness* looking for the potential of the collective.

After these experiences (intellectual, artistic, and activist), we may conclude the anthropophagical task is to deal with possible realities without restricting them to a priori categories, but to search for the activation of movements. In a radical way, anthropophagy can even destabilize the notion of alterity or otherness, by proposing multiplicities or pluralities.

In the history of Western philosophy and science, this devouring operation can be recognized by other names. They are not exactly the same, but came from a similar attempt to disclose the precarious and discontinuous nature of the self. I'm thinking about the transduction proposed by Gilbert Simondon, the radical pragmatism of William James, the arachnid movements of Fernand Deligny, the enaction of Francisco Varela, and the minor movements of Brian Massumi and Erin Manning, among others. In the artistic field, scholars working with performing arts (e.g. Lepecki 2016, Cvejić 2015)[24] have been proposing artistic creation as a process that operates for and as differentiation. In these contexts, the epistemologies of shamanism and anthropophagy seem to be much more than exotic ways of thinking, or poetical tools. They should be considered an original perspective to problematize the neoliberal rationality and the illusion of autonomous subjects who seem to be eternally condemned to dream of their own lives.

Notes

1   I have developed this idea of otherness
    as a state of creation in my book
    *Fabulações do corpo japonês e seus
    microativismos* (Fabulations of the
    Japanese Body and its Microactivisms)
    (São Paulo: ed. n-1, 2017). Through
    neoliberal economic policies,
    otherness is something to be avoided
    or tolerated—which according to
    Wendy Brown is a current discourse
    of depoliticization (*Regulating
    Aversion: Tolerance in the Age of Identity
    and Empire* [Princeton: Princeton
    University Press, 2006]). Strategies
    such as anthropophagy and fabulation
    can give us another perspective to
    deal with otherness as an operator to
    create something else, such as a flux
    of thinking-feelings, a dislocation of
    time-space, and sometimes a political
    disclosure of worlds never meant to
    appear.

2   Jacques Derrida, *Spectres de Marx:
    L'État de la dette, le travail du deuil et la
    nouvelle Internationale* (Paris: Galilée,
    1993).

3   Some discussions conducted by
    Antonio Negri, Michael Hardt,
    Slavoj Žižek and Paolo Virno could
    be considered as post-marxist
    articulations or possible answers for
    hypothetical tasks, by concerning for
    example the notions of multitude and
    immaterial labour.

4   Some of the most notable participants
    were painters such as Anita Malfatti,
    Emiliano Di Cavalcanti, Vicente
    do Rego Monteiro, Inácio da Costa
    Ferreira, and Victor Brecheret; writers
    such as Oswald de Andrade, Mário
    de Andrade, Sérgio Milliet, Plínio
    Salgado, Menotti del Picchia, Ronald
    de Carvalho, Guilherme de Almeida,
    and Álvaro Moreira; musicians such as
    Heitor Villa-Lobos, Guiomar Novais,
    and Ernani Braga, among others.

5   In many ways, this plan has been very
    successful. The presence of more than
    thirty foreign countries (each with a
    specific pavilion or representative)
    highlighted the potential of Brazil,
    which at that time was considered
    to be the great exponent of Latin
    America.

6   Tupi is the linguistic family of the
    Tupi-Guarani tribe, which was one of
    the largest tribes in Brazil, spanning
    thirteen states, before becoming nearly
    extinct through successive attacks.

7   Oswald Andrade, 'Mensagem ao
    Antropófago Desconhecido' (1946),
    in *Estética e Política* (Rio de Janeiro:
    Editora Globo, 1991), pp. 285–286.

8   Eduardo Viveiros de Castro,
    Metafísicas Canibais (São Paulo: ed.
    n-1, 2015).

9   Eduardo Viveiros de Castro, *A
    Inconstância da alma selvagem e outros
    ensaios de antropologia* (São Paulo:
    Cosac Naify, 2002).

10 Davi Kopenawa and Bruce Albert,
    *The Falling Sky: Words of a Yanomani
    Shaman*, trans. Nicholas Elliot and
    Alison Dundy (Cambridge, MA:
    Harvard University Press, 2013).

11 Homi K. Bhabha, *The Location of
    Culture* (New York: Routledge, 2004).

12 Edward Said, *Orientalism* (New York:
    Vintage, 1979).

13 Chimamanda Ngozi Adichie, *We
    Should All Be Feminists* (New York:
    Anchor Book, 2015).

14 The 2013 protests in Brazil started as
    the Movimento Passe Livre (Free Fare
    Movement) asking for cheaper public
    transportation. However, other issues
    came up during the protests, such
    as questions related to racism and
    gender; and it became the biggest mass
    movement since the impeachment of
    President Fernando Color de Mello in
    1992.

15 Suely Rolnik, *Esferas da Insurreição:
    Notas para uma vida não cafetinada*
    (São Paulo: ed. n-1, 2018).

16 Suely Rolnik, 'Politics of Flexible
    Subjectivity: The Event Work of
    Lygia Clark', in *Antinomies of Art
    and Culture*, eds. Terry Smith,
    Okwui Enwezor and Nancy Condee
    (Durham, NC: Duke University Press,
    2008, pp. 97–112).

17 Susan Sontag's book *Regarding the
    Pain of Others* reverses the terms she
    sets out in 1977 in *On Photography*.
    Arguing instead for an interpretation
    of images that reveals their ability
    to inspire violence or create
    apathy, she evokes a long history
    of the representation of the pain of
    others—from Goya's *The Disasters
    of War* (1810–1820) to photographic
    documents of the American Civil
    War, World War I, the Spanish Civil
    War, the Nazi death camps, and
    contemporary images from Bosnia,
    Sierra Leone, Rwanda, Israel and
    Palestine, and New York City on
    September 11.

18 Kopenawa and Albert, *The Falling Sky.*

19 Thomas Lemke, *Biopolitics an Advanced Introduction* (New York: University Press, 2011). Esposito, Roberto *Bios, Biopolitics and Philosophy* Translated by Timothy Campbell (Minneapolis: Minnesota University Press, 2008).

20 Antonio Negri and Michael Hardt, *Empire* (Cambridge, MA: Harvard University Press, 2000); Antonio Negri and Michael Hardt, *Multitude: War and Democracy in the Age of Empire* (London: Penguin Press, 2004).

21 Núcleo do Dirceu participants in this project were Allexandre Santos, Caio César, César Costa, Cleyde Silva, Elielson Pacheco, Humilde Alves, Izabelle Frota, Jell Carone, Jacob Alves, Janaína Lobo, Layane Holanda, Marcelo Evelin, Regina Veloso e Soraya Portela.

22 See www.demolitionincorporada.com/1000casas.

23 *1000 Casas* (São Paulo: Itaú Cultural, 2012).

24 André Lepecki, *Singularities: Dance in the Age of Performance* (London: Routledge, 2016); Bojana Cvejić , *Choreographing Problems. Expressive Concepts in Contemporary Dance and Performance* (London: Palgrave, 2015).

Beyond the Either-Or of Monoculture and Multiculture
Transformative Practices from Eurasia

Mi You

At what scale can we address monoculture, and its opposite, poly-culture or heteroculture? If monoculture is rare in biology, even in a small patch of land, how can we investigate monoculturalism in culture? Here, it seems that before we recognize our embeddedness in a monoculture, we almost always have drawn the boundaries and created the monoculture to start with—consciously or unknowingly because of inheritance or the 'natural' appearance of it. From national identity discourses to Big Tech's monopolies in our daily lives, and ultimately capitalism's creed of efficiency and optimization as the only desirable and feasible value system, monocultural discourses prevail in multiple forms.

In the biosphere, monoculture is vulnerable to invasive species. Can we say the same for the social sphere? Pyotr Kropotkin (1849–1921), the Russian founder of anarcho-communism, was a geographer before he turned social anarchist. He spent years in Siberia studying the flora and fauna, as well as geological formations there. He contributed to the study of biology by proposing the idea of 'mutual aid' instead of the Darwinian 'survival of the fittest' as the principle underlying evolution. The curious migration of forms of organization from the biological world to the social realm was not merely coincidental. Kropotkin befriended the French anarchist geographer Élisée Reclus (1830–1905), who, at the height of scientific explorations of Central Asia during the second half of the nineteenth century, when cartography serviced the military and designs of roads and railways met the interest of capitalists, saw geology and geography being mined for geopolitical leverage. Reclus attempted to write the story of the earth and of humanity as one, or as he terms it, the story of 'nature becoming self-conscious'. Integral to this history is an account of the forces of domination that emerge in human history, only to restrict the future self-realization of both humanity and nature (Clark 2013, p. 6). Both anarchist geographers explored the parallel territories of movements in the natural world and social movements and attempted to shift the emphasis on social domination through creating self-organized bodies of communities. They saw class struggle, the search for equilibrium and the sovereign decision of the individual as the basic underpinnings (Jun and Wahl 2010, p. 221).

Eurasianism and *Tianxia*

If we think turning to the opposite of monoculture is an easy solution to the problem, then we might be trapped in another set of problems. Just like monoculture, multiculturalism comes in many forms. The history of global trade, going back to as early as the ancient times, provides us with rich evidence of cultural transfers, manifested in syncretic artistic forms, religious practices, and lifestyles. My own research on the Silk Roads, the historical networks in Eurasia and beyond, especially testifies to this. One can dedicate a lifetime of investigation into the migration of form of the Buddhist icons throughout Asia. It is also true, however, that people in history have often held prejudices against each other. For example, the Arabs considered the crusaders savages and the Chinese designated the various nomadic peoples as barbaric. What differentiates this from modern racism is the latter's perpetuation of violence and exploitation in institutionalized forms.

And what is at stake, when we reach back to history for ideas, inspiration, or evidence? It is not enough to see the Silk Roads as a pre-modern decentralized and global network, as if what motivates us to dive into the deep past is only to find evidence for structures and networks existing today. We know all too well how global trade networks reinforce the dominance of capitalistic conglomerates, beyond the cultural aspects of globalization. We also know that decentralized networks of the modern era grew out of the military communication context with Paul Baran designing a 'survivable' network for the Rand Corporation in the 1960s. The Silk Roads are not just a set of decentralized networks by virtue of its spatial distribution, much more important is the distribution of power—no single polity or entity dominated the trade network. We are not going back to the Silk Road to find what has always been there, but the bigger question is, to what extent can we be inspired by it and distil certain practices that may harbour transformative potential for the future society, and help us co-exist in contemporary society today? The past and the future are folded into each other through practical models of transformations.

Here, I will first discuss how seemingly inclusive and heterogeneous thinking systems can, if misused, be just as exclusionary as monocultural discourses. I will draw on the example of Eurasianism and *tianxia*.

Long before the construction of the Trans-Siberian Railroad between 1892 and 1905, Prince Vladimir Odoevsky's science fiction novel *The Year 4338*, composed in the 1830s, described an 'electrical railroad' running from Peking to St. Petersburg via tunnels under the Himalayas and the Caspian Sea. Though seemingly timid in vision when compared to science fiction novels about space travel, *The Year 4338* was in fact rather ambitious, considering that Russia had only begun building modest-length railroads in 1836, while the electrical railroad was invented much later. In the novel, the railroad put Czarist Russia in the centre of the world, whereas Britain, France, and Germany's positions were greatly diminished. In this regard, Odoevsky's novel is one of the earliest contributions to Classical Eurasianism, an intellectual movement that tried to establish a unique, self-sufficient cultural space for Russia, distinct from Western Europe and embracing its Eastern roots (Banerjee 2013, pp. 25–28).

Classical Eurasianism emerged in the 1920s as a theory that claimed full cultural relativism, acknowledging the opacities and differences of cultures in the context of a critique of Western dominance. Each geo-cultural space has its unique characteristics and should develop its own path to modernity, as opposed to following the steps of the West—this was deemed European cultural hegemony. At the time, the world appeared to the Classical Eurasianists as broken up into territorial cells with relatively hermetic geo-cultures. One of them was Russia-Eurasia, the supranational geo-culture united under the self-identification of Russia with its Eastern traits while sharing a common destiny, and—similarly to Western Europe, India, or the USA—with its own significance and specificity (Glebov 2017). In some ways, the Eurasianists anticipated later postcolonial discourses based on cultural relativism and strategic essentialism that were advanced by theorists Dipesh Chakrabarty and Gayatri Spivak, and others (Smirnov 2019), and, most alarmingly, the re-surfacing of the right-wing 'Eurasian' movement today, headed by Russian political strategist Aleksandr Dugin. Dugin's support for the Eurasia Party movement since the 2000s borrows the intellectual resources of Eurasianism in fashioning an Anti-American, yet in effect neo-imperial Russian political movement. Mired in muddled geo-politics, Dugin's Eurasianism celebrates Russia's expansionist agenda to build a Eurasian sphere of influence, using the ocean and continent as a metaphor to describe a continental grounding associated with Eurasia, and to condemn liberal intellectuals for following the water—the Pacific—and looking West.

Science fiction, more than mere speculation on the not-yet-there, can sometimes actively shape the look of the future. In the case of *The Year 4338*, it is the geographical imagination built on geo-cultural determination in tandem with technological speculation that heralds a host of 'science non-fictions'—the era of accelerated expansionism, military campaigns, and the Great Game, all informing geopolitics of Central and East Asia until today.

Geographical imagination is deeply embedded in the political claims on Eurasia. The ideology that fuelled Japan's expansionism before and during World War II was Pan-Asianism, under which the plan for a 'Greater East Asia Co-prosperity Sphere' was drawn: an economic, cultural and political collective-entity encompassing parts of north-east Asia and Southeast Asia. With the rhetoric of brotherhood and common culture, the nations were to get rid of the rule of European colonial powers under the guidance of Japan. On the material level, infrastructure played an important role. The gargantuan infrastructure projects undertaken or planned by the Japanese and in cooperation with their partners saw the development of railway connections from Japan to Western Europe and throughout Southeast Asia.

In a different register, the Confucian world order of *tianxia*, which means 'everything under heaven', historically denotes a hierarchical world system whereby the Chinese Empire was at the centre, with countries on the periphery entering into a tributary relationship with China. This could be observed in the interaction between China and its neighbouring states well until the early modern era. Though theoretically unequal, the tributary system afforded a degree of informal equality to tribute states as it allowed for fair exchange and trade driven by the self-interests of the parties involved. A further political and geopolitical consequence was that the tributary system enabled greater security for those involved without engaging in arms races (Kang 2010, p. 55). In this way, the system contributed to the peaceful co-existence of different peoples and polities—an idea that extends into the Belt and Road Initiative (BRI), a platform that China launched in 2013 to interlink China with regions along the ancient Silk Road and the maritime trade routes connecting East Asia to Africa and Europe.

The BRI's mandate is to promote and facilitate regional multilateral cooperation. To date, the initiative has expanded to around seventy countries in Asia, the Middle East, Africa, Europe and Oceania, incorporating one-third of global GDP and one-quarter of global foreign investment flows (Zecha et al. 2016), However, concerns over 'debt trap' were raised and cases of bad

loans have led to severe political circumstances. When the Sri Lankan government failed to pay back the debt to the Chinese lender in 2015, it sold a 99-year lease to China Merchant Ports Holdings granting rights to the Hambantota Port. Recent studies reveal that China's leverage remained limited and, in many cases, the renegotiation resolved in favour of the borrower (Pilling 2019). When China came in the spotlight at the World Economic Forum in 2017 as a defender of globalization, vis-à-vis protectionism and retractions in the 'free world', the political ideology of *tianxia* captured the imagination across different political camps.

The pre-modern Silk Road and BRI are often mentioned in the same breath, conflating old and new geographical imaginations. Concurrently, there is a surge of scholarship on *tianxia* as (old and new) imperial China's world order—Zhao Tingyang, for example, has argued for *tianxia* as an ideal form of global governance beyond 'international politics', based on the harmony and common wellbeing of all peoples (Zhao 2009, pp. 5–18). Scholar Cai Menghan has brought caveats to the generalization of the term by tracing its usage. Importantly, Cai has shown that *tianxia* discourses faded in the Song and Ming dynasties, until reviving in the early Qing dynasty around mid-seventeenth century in the contemporary debate surrounding the fall of the country versus the demise of the *tianxia*. It was believed that the Manchu overlords may conquer China, but they could never triumph over the *tianxia* (Cai 2017). This seems to suggest *tianxia*, at that particular moment in early Qing Dynasty, encapsulates a Chinese culturalist, albeit emancipatory proto-nationalism. This shows the curious careers of both *tianxia* and Eurasia, that they may harbour emancipatory potential at times, point to peaceful coexistence and global governance at others, while also being co-opted to justify neo-imperial practices.

Hence, we need to practice a thinking-cartography that follows a to-and-fro movement, which means it sometimes contradicts in order to affirm on a different level, or vice versa. As seen here, we move between affirming multiculturalism and critically reassessing it in a shifted context. Or, when it comes to the understanding of Asian or nomadic cosmologies, temporalities, and social dynamics, we move between confirming and contradicting differences, for simply affirming 'indigenous' thinking as post-colonialist critique may veil other forms of self-orientalization and cultural elitism. The thinking process takes both the motion of deconstruction (in a negative-productive way) and dynamitic transformation, which entails a recursive process of regress and as such is open to reconsideration and revision. This is perhaps the skill of equestrian archery perfected by the historical nomads, which involves riding a horse, aiming at a moving subject, and shooting with a bow and arrow, constituting a meta-stable state amidst multiple movements, or a premodern constant feedback loop.

Unmapping Eurasia

Now, if monoculture is problematic and the overarching narratives on multiculturalism can be co-opted, how can we not be trapped by the either-or of multiculturalism? How can we approach multiculture from below?

Unmapping Eurasia is a long-term art and transcultural study and project initiated by the director of the Casco Art Institute: Working for the Commons, Binna Choi, and myself. It proposes to unlearn what has obstructed Eurasian visions and practices, from the coloniality at play on both sides of the colonialist spectrum to the Cold War's constructed opposition between communism and capitalism, and the various claims on Eurasia mentioned above. More importantly, this study focuses on and enacts old and new polycentric movements for commoning, ways of thinking and living, and social systems operating within the principle of the commons. The inspiration of *Unmapping Eurasia* comes from the Eurasian nomads, travellers, and 'time divers' who make up a transhistorical speculative cartography. The project evolves as different geographies are interwoven together through various modes of 'movement', including long-term research and study programmes, performative symposiums, artistic commissions and exhibitions, and infrastructural research with other socio-political agents—all while being open to emerging practices, sensitivities, and ecologies.

Our proposal for unmapping can be considered alongside the line of possibility, while not without 'embracing' mapping. We are not mapping over other maps, but we look at or create one map after another, by reading their lines, their methods, and the minds and nature behind them; namely the logics of power. In mapping, we may search for multiple versions of cartographic representations of a place and, above all, for other mapping methods before modern cartography: using a tree branch to draw on the sand, yes, that method of 'the savage' as the colonial geographer called it; song lyrics passed on through recitals, spiritual journeys conflated with mountain landscape drawings and again conflated with the human body, star atlases on petroglyphs dotted throughout Eurasia's steppes and deserts. Here, maps are for collective movement and serve as navigational tools for minds to sail together. Often, these maps situate the mover in a cosmos that moves with them instead of rendering the space static for the explorer to return to it—a commons shared between the mover and the space.

Unmapping is a method of mapping against universal objectivity and its pose of completeness, knowingness, and domination. Unmapping celebrates the positions of each one who maps and makes these positions visible while drawing connections and highlighting interdependence among them. This comes with the refusal to judge, although evaluation is appreciated. The maps from unmapping are hence manifold, sporadic, and ephemeral.

One beautiful moment of unmapping Eurasia emerged as we explored different methods of approaching the heart of Eurasia with our students at the Dutch Art Institute. The heart of Eurasia is a place, or non-place imbued with myths, histories, and political intentions. Nursultan Nazarbayev, who served as the first President of Kazakhstan from 1990 to March 2019, published a book entitled *Heart of Eurasia* to place the country in the region, but the Eurasian heart beats loudly and cannot be confined by Kazakhstan's borders. There are the Pamir Mountains, the Himalayas, the Hindu Kush, the Tianshan, and the Altai, across southern Siberia, Central Asia and western China, as if a body has no use to be apart and the organs operate through the connective tissues, veins and nerves.

The attempt to be in touch with the Eurasian heart without geopolitical borders instead led us to the notion of 'navel'—or the navel of Eurasia—to redefine 'navel gazing'. The navel of our body grumbles with a low pitch, just like the earth underneath us, only discernible by listening up close.

Our students started dreaming of the belly-button conference that channels our bodily knowledge and mediates it with that of the Continent. It is a place of myth, created as you lie on another person's belly and listen through its button. It may not be a coincidence that the Hundun, or 'chaos', the emperor in the middle realm and a faceless being in Chinese mythic-geography *Shan Hai Jing* (*Book of Mountains and Seas*) and then introduced in the fable by Zhuangzi, is geographically located somewhere near the navel point of Eurasia. Hundun died as it was offered seven holes in its body—eyes, ears, nostrils and a mouth—by two of its guests, one from the north and another from the south, who thought of them as a gift back for the incredible hospitality of Hundun (it is said that Hundun was a great dancer). This myth warns of the risk of our perceptual or even sensorial distinction, its cost to life that is hospitable chaos over the order. It then overlaps with a tragic drama: Semey (formerly Semipalatinsk), also known as 'The Seven Chambered City' is situated at the navel of the Eurasian landmass, in eastern Kazakhstan, and was built upon the ruins of a Buddhist monastery. Once it was a major crossroads for trade between the nomadic peoples of Central Asia and the Russian Empire and it connected with the Silk Road. Later, between 1949 and 1989, it was used as a nuclear testing site before being turned into a student town filled with scientists. The remnants of rockets, when dropping back to earth, tended to land in the steppes of Central Asia. Not far from there, the Crater of Fire in the Karakum Desert in Turkmenistan, caused by oil drilling and unstoppable gas leakage, has been burning for almost 50 years.

These engagements go beyond the confines of Eurasia's modern cultural cartography, which is based on national and cultural attributions and delineations. At the same time, they are not taken literally or merely as curious objects of archaeological and art historical relevance. Rather, they constitute speculative and materialist engagements with agency that entails different scales of critique and action, while in negotiation with themselves. In the deep-time, deep-space connections in Eurasia, we can unearth much that can inspire us today.

Practical Examples of Transformation from Eurasia

I have often seen metallic jewellery and ornament produced by historical nomadic and semi-nomadic peoples on the Steppes. It was also the case with bronze objects from the Kulay culture, which populated the region between 500 BCE–500 CE in the local history museum in Tomsk in central Siberia. However, one object was of special interest: a cauldron for casting metal. It is a meta-object that conditions the production of all the other bronze objects. The nomads attached fibulas, gold or silver plaques and pieces of jewellery to small movable objects. Not only were the resulting objects easy to transport, they also 'pertain to the object only as object in motion', write Gilles Deleuze and Félix Guattari.

'These plaques constitute traits of expression of pure speed, carried on objects that are themselves mobile and moving' (Deleuze and Guattari 1987, p. 401).

The continuous motion and constant necessity of recasting according to needs render the objects beyond the form and content demarcation as often applied in art history. Rather, the objects are in the process of rebalancing and mutual mutation. Taking this negotiation between being part of a continuous flow of matters and energy and the individuation process works as a metaphor for the social, could we not ask: what if we do not regard the individual as discrete entities but as changing composites of all the social forces? How can we engage in meaningful ways as part of a larger community beyond individualist interests while not being struck by the fear of losing oneself? Why are we afraid of losing oneself, when in fact we are so lonely in contemporary society?

Or take another set of objects, the petroglyphs. The prehistorical petroglyphs span multiple eras—iron age, bronze age, and later the Turkic period. They have been sometimes marked over, a prehistorical palimpsest wherein the annotations may or may not share the same semantical system. It's hard to imagine that ancient men would have the consecrated image of archaeology we have today, or any functional understanding of periodization, for that matter. So imagine the iron era men looking at the bronze era human and animal figures, what would they be thinking?

What happens is a set of self-motivated activities, copying, imitating, inventing new forms, and marking them down. Of course, certain elements may be passed on through other media, such as shamanic ritual traditions (shaman figures are found in petroglyphs in various locations, which exhibit ostensibly similar features as practices until today). The existing markings from the forerunners provide a certain conditioning to their world.

On the network organizational level, this reminds me—in a very speculative way—of textual games of MUD/MUSH/MOO culture (online multiuser, interactive textual game), where in a decentralized space, any player can modify the game by coding a certain environment, and that environment will be changed for the other users. ('Look around the room', 'there are objects XYZ...', 'Take object X'. And for the next gamer to enter this room there will be only object YZ. Most importantly, gamers can code things—'change gravity at a location', and all other players will be subjected to the new gravity condition there.) This kind of games were the pre-life to now massive multiplayer online games (and afterlife of RPG without the game master), but function in a de-centralized fashion that includes the self-sustained design/emergence of the game itself. A collective speculation of worlds and the wording of such worlds. In the MUSH games, the speculation is across space, more or less at the same time. In the petroglyphs, they are across space and time—a global, distributed tarot card game without a game master, or distributed memes.

Taking the petroglyphs as an allegory for value and organizational systems instead of being fixated on their art historical meanings, we could see that this reading of the petroglyphs as a decentralized game (not just in storage but in its process) highlights the inherently creative character of the situation: what you do in a game comes from what you could offer or contribute to the world, which has a subjective and idiosyncratic value, a value of its own. If we imagine a social form based on such value forms, we could start reprogramming the economy and create economies of abundance and diversity, not tied to the monoculture of capitalism.

All of these transhistorical reflections resonate with what Félix Guattari sees as the ethico-political extensions of the fractalization of the psyche, which disrupts 'the destiny of the one-dimensionality of the capitalistic subjectivation', and can 'cause its own eviction by heterogeneous, multicentred, polyphonic, polyvocal approaches, installing itself outside pre-coded equilibriums' (Guattari 1987, p. 85).

This meta-balance while resolutely being on the move is an allegory of our time, if we could all accept that returning to static and fixed identities and narratives is not impossible. An alternate understanding of our own multitude and of the multitude of our social forms is possible, if we plunge into the Eurasian deep-time, deep-space connections. Horizontal, vertical, and temporary axes are not spatialized, absolute coordinates, but can be conflated into each other, and at their convergence we see mythical stories and 'indigenous' practices emerging, but we also observe the undulating transformation networks, matters and energies returning in different forms. We learn to be guided by histories, stories and practical models from below in Eurasia and adapt them to our time—even if we can only start with ourselves and small communities around us.

References

— Banerjee, Anindita. 2013. *We Modern People: Science Fiction and the Making of Russian Modernity*. Middletown: Wesleyan University Press.

— Cai, Menghan. 2017. '论天下——超越天下主义的困境 [On Tianxia: Overcoming the Delimma of tianxia].' 文化纵横 Beijing Cultural Review.

— Clark, John. 2013. 'Introduction'. In *Anarchy, Geography, Modernity Selected Writings of Elisée Reclus*, eds. John Clark and Martin Camille. Oakland: PM Press.

— Deleuze, Gilles, and Félix Guattari. 1987. *A Thousand Plateaus: Capitalism & Schizophrenia*. Minneapolis: University of Minnesota Press.

— Glebov, Sergey. 2017. *From Empire to Eurasia: Politics, Scholarship, and Ideology in Russian Eurasianism, 1920s–1930s*. DeKalb: Northern Illinois University Press.

— Guattari, Félix. 1987. 'Cracks in the Street'. *Flash Art* 135, pp. 82–85.

— Jun, Nathan, and Shane Wahl, eds. 2010. *New Perspectives on Anarchism* (Lanham, MD: Lexington Books).

— Kang, David C. 2010. *East Asia Before the West: Five Centuries of Trade and Tribute*. New York: Columbia University Press.

— Pilling, David. 2019. 'It Is Wrong to Demonise Chinese Labour Practices in Africa'. *Financial Times*, 3 July.

— Smirnov, Nikolay. 2019. 'Left-Wing Eurasianism and Postcolonial Theory'. *e-flux* 97.

— Zecha, Cecilia Ma, et al. 2016. 'China's One Belt, One Road: Will It Reshape Global Trade?' *McKinsey podcast*.

— Zhao, Tingyang. 2009. 'A Political World Philosophy in Terms of All-Under-Heaven (Tian-xia)'. *Diogenes* 56, no. 1, pp. 5–18.

Proxies, with a Life of Their Own

Iman Issa

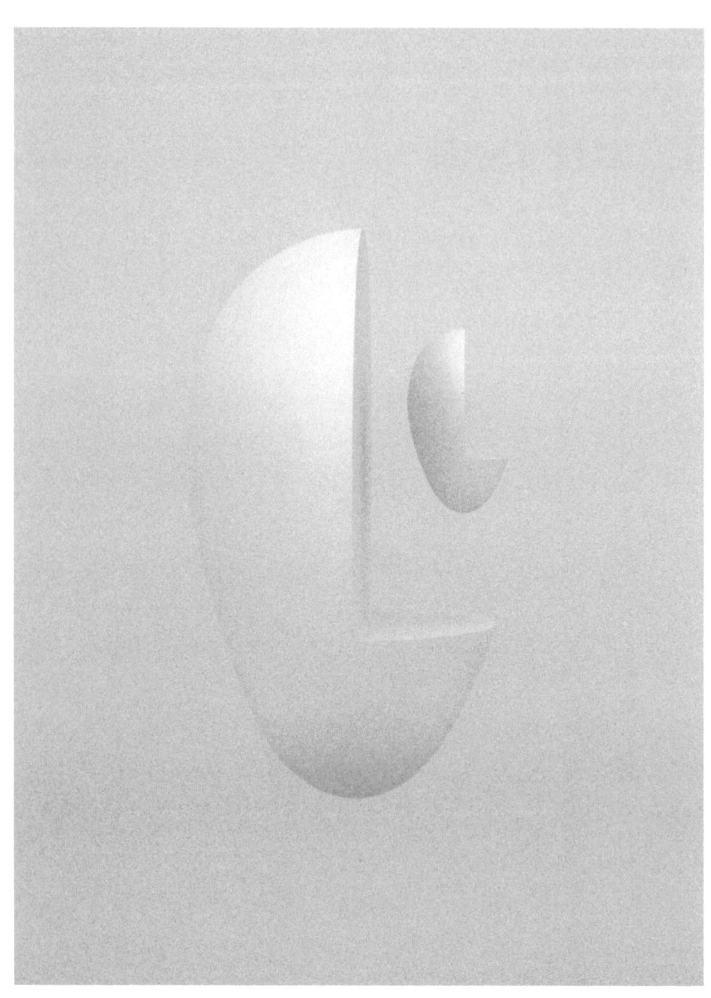

The Aesthetics of Ambiguity

166

Self-Portrait
Self as William S. Burroughs who suggested that if we implanted
electrodes directly into the brain and could control it absolutely,
there would be nothing left to control.

Iman Issa

167

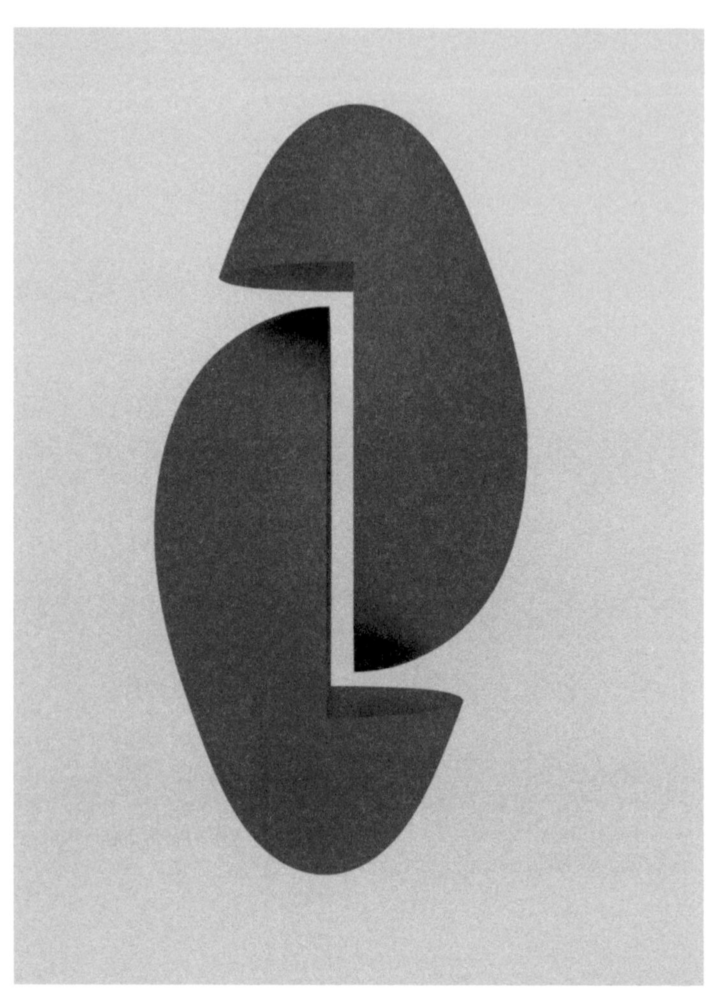

Self-Portrait
Self as Doria Shafik who repeatedly asserted, in her texts,
speeches, lectures, and interviews, that being a woman was
absolutely (no) different from being a man.

Iman Issa

169

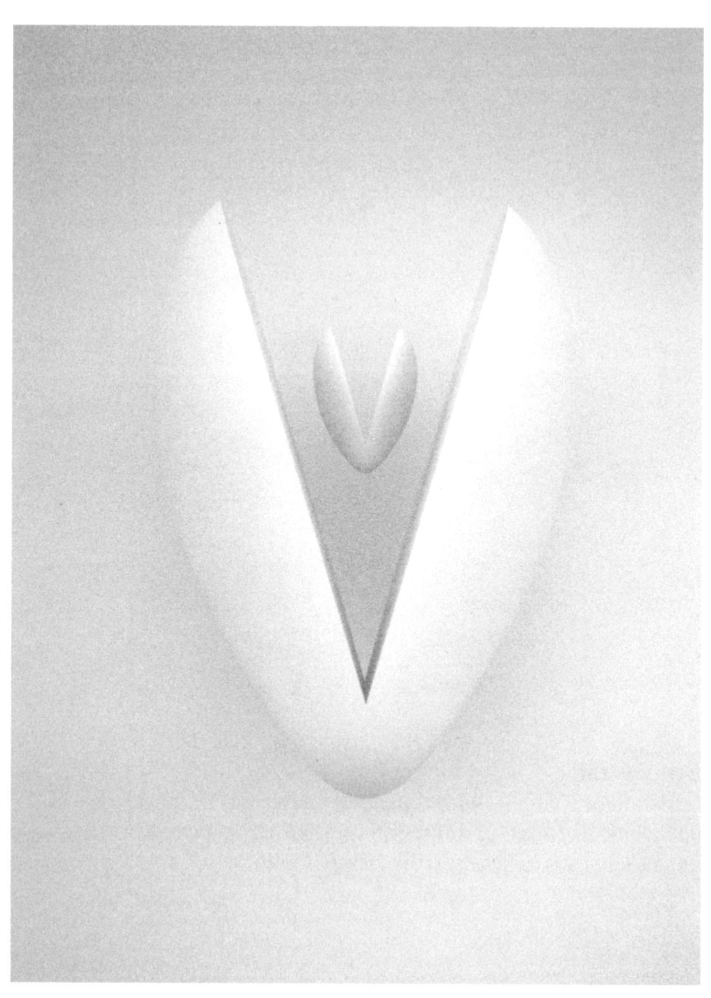

Self-Portrait
Self as Alenka Zupančič who recounted the joke: 'There are no
cannibals here. We ate the last one yesterday.'

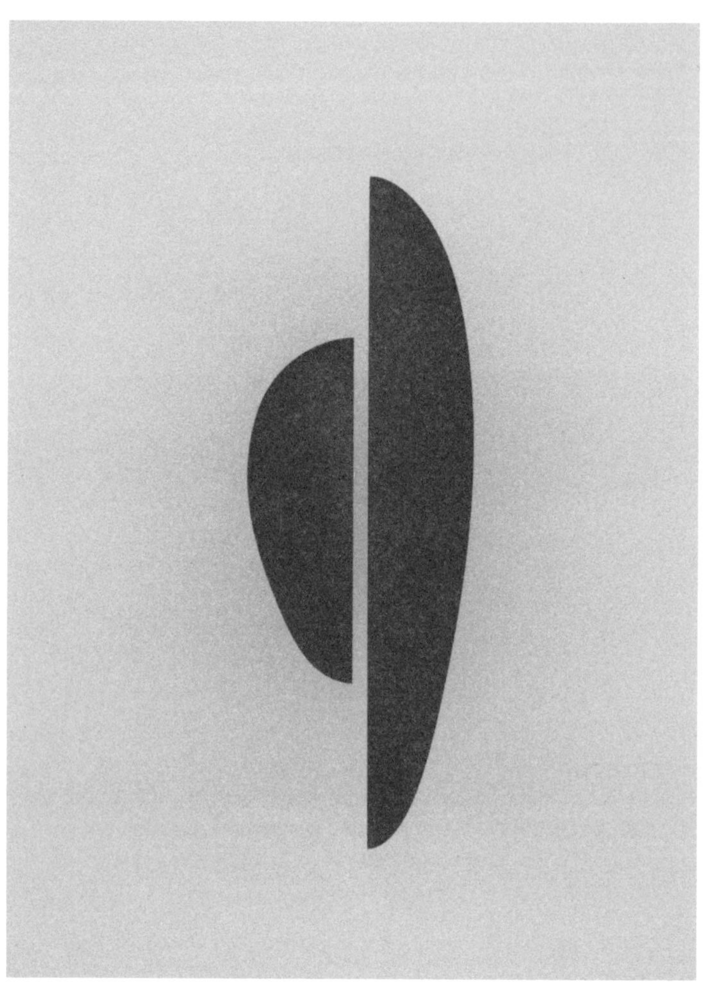

172

Self-Portrait
Self as Taha Hussein who referred to himself in the third person,
and who often divided his observations between those sensed
from his right and left, respectively.

Iman Issa

173

Proxies, with a Life of Their Own, is an ongoing project by Iman Issa, composed of a number of self-portraits. All the portraits are variations on a single initial shape of a generic head.

List of plates in order of appearance:
Self-Portrait: Self as William S. Burroughs, 2019
Self-Portrait: Self as Doria Shafik, 2020
Self-Portrait: Self as Alenka Zupančič, 2020
Self-Portrait: Self as Taha Hussein, 2020

Iman Issa

175

A General Sort of Aversion to the 'Aboutness' of Things

Nav Haq in conversation with Tirdad Zolghadr

Tirdad Zolghadr is a writer and curator based in Berlin. His book *Traction* (Sternberg, 2016) looks at the condition of contemporary art today, arguing that art has become defined by a moral economy of indeterminacy. Reflecting on experiences in his own work, as well as on the work of others, he considers the positioning of artistic, curatorial, and institutional work, and the tendency towards constant deferment or defusing of a statement, or of situating oneself, depriving art of its potential for real change.

> It was only slowly that I woke up to the stakes at hand, and noticed that only few things hold as much potential as our tentacular milieu, but also that few things are quite as hampered by our own escapism. Today, I am increasingly bored to tears by contemporary art, but I still have more faith in its potentials than anyone I know.

Nav Haq, one of the editors of this book, invited him for a conversation to discuss his ideas, share their thoughts on institutional work, and to compare Zolghadr's call for a more 'didactic' future in relation to Haq's viewpoint on the need for art to provide experiences with ambiguity.

Nav Haq

To kick off the conversation, I thought it would make sense for you to give an introduction to the ideas you lay out in your book *Traction*, which questions 'indeterminacy' in contemporary art. What do you mean by 'indeterminacy', and how do you feel it contributes to the undermining of contemporary art's potential?

Tirdad Zolghadr

I'll try and do that as briefly as I can. Let's start with something that brings the two of us together. We worked on a long research and exhibition project called *Lapdogs of the Bourgeoisie.*[1] And it had a lot of qualities and strengths to show for itself. But at the end of the day, we both felt we had invested a lot of time in the questions we raised, on the topic of class in the artworld, and then walked away. Without putting the expertise we had accumulated to the test. And without trying to set up hypotheses to understand what the answers to our questions might have been. I realized, round about that time, that I had actually worked on several projects that were similar. A lot of sincerity, a lot of blood, sweat, and tears invested in really long-term projects. And then this sense of, well, what would be a punchy way to put it? A sense of not really honouring one's own specialization. Not taking oneself seriously enough. Preferring to leave it open and walk away to the next thing. Then someone who worked on *Lapdogs of the Bourgeoisie* with us, Suhail Malik, came up with a set of hypotheses as to why this type of thing is not a coincidence, but actually central to how contemporary art works. We do not develop answers to the questions that we raise because this would supposedly impede the sort of creativity we treasure. It would compromise what we think makes contemporary art interesting to begin with. Contemporary art insists on an encounter with the audience that is unpredictable to the point of renewing itself with every one of those encounters. That is ideally so incommensurable that no two encounters are the same. This is what we work towards. Now, this is something I wholeheartedly subscribed to for a long time, and that I still get a kick out of in terms of a private experience. I go to a museum. I see art and I dig it.

But I also see limitations to this. For one, we keep starting from zero. We could not accumulate expertise through our *Lapdogs* thing. We had to leave it open and walk away. We couldn't be so preposterous as to say we have positions here and there. We start from zero again and again. That's one problem. The second is that it's not entirely realistic. Dig deeper and you realize all this open-endedness is not even open-ended. You actually do put positions on the table, even if you pretend they're just questions. Inspirational innuendos. Open invitations to the audience's creativity. When actually, what is put on the table is a mainstream liberal take on things, aesthetically, politically, intellectually, epistemologically speaking. Let's take *Lapdogs* again. People who walked into the shows would walk away with a very particular aesthetic experience that is actually not that crazy. What they took in was a finely honed political argument, an intuitively centre-left take on class relationships. The type which, you know, sees outright conflict as a bit too dramatic. But then outright quietism is a bit too conservative. So, you settle for reformist suggestions regarding conditions of production, very carefully. If at least we had spelled it out as such. Instead we stylized and aestheticized it, and put it out there as a set of questions. *Traction* tries to unravel this knot and propose other scenarios.

NH

In terms of what I've been working on around ambiguity, whilst, I might add, oblivious to what you have been doing on indeterminacy, I feel we're coming from different angles, but I think they're not necessarily incompatible. I share your thoughts about the condition of art, and its limitations. It's interesting you started with *Lapdogs of the Bourgeoisie*. I'm reminded of when we presented the project in Istanbul, where we also held a public event. There was a group of students, and one of them asked us a question at one point, which I think is relevant here because the question was: why not just look at this issue of class from a scientific perspective—undertake some sort of field analysis, gather some data, draw some conclusions and use all that. I don't think we really gave an adequate answer to it. But I suppose maybe one reason is that unlike, say, a scientific experiment, people don't think of artistic work as being a means to an end in the same way as a scientific experiment. I'm perplexed in the question of why exactly it's like this. I think, reading your book, you have a hypothesis where you're saying that the art world is somehow trying to embody the conditions of globalization—this all-encompassing complexity. I do think that is part of it, as well as there being a general sort of aversion to the 'aboutness' of things. I'm also wondering if it's also a kind of anti-modern attitude? You suggest early on in your book that it isn't to do with a 1990's post-modern approach of cultural relativism. I myself feel there might be a bit of that still. I do think that over the last twenty years there has been a process of internationalization as well as an awareness of stereotypes or a false dichotomy, between 'East' and 'West'—the West being about rationality, and the East being about intuition—and trying to be mindful of this. Mindfulness as trying not to be Eurocentric, I suppose. And so, anti-modern in that sense.

TZ

I'll try to take your question very literally, and answer it if I can. One reason why it's like that, if I were to make an educated guess, is that, as you say yourself, contemporary art allows us to mirror globalization. To assemble absolutely anything that is worthy of note, or useful, or inspiring, within the room, at the spur of the moment, without summoning the kind of checks and balances and expertise that is usually demanded of such an exercise. After all, it's about being contemporary, as in contemporary art, nothing more, nothing less. It's not about folkloric art, abstract art, therapeutic art. A new moment, a new quasi-presence. Again and again and again. And if that's all it is, then it's also innocent. So, you don't have to worry about it, not in the way you would worry about science. If there's a scientific ambition, people get a little more suspicious. Where are your references from? How are you so confident about what you're saying? But if you're engaging in this indeterminate experiment that reinvents itself with every audience encounter, there is an innocence at play. Which in turn gives you an enormous moral leeway. A license to travel far and wide. This is one reason why our field is successful, and why it is defined the way it is. The other reason is historical. Some trace it back to Kant. I'm not going to do that because it would take too long and because my footing in this is not as solid as it should be. So, I do not talk Kant. But if you look at modernism as you mentioned it, at how modernism was defined by authoritarian figures such as the critic, the professor, the master artist, and you look at the hunger to get rid of those fuckers cementing those Eurocentric hierarchies, well in Euroamerica you can spot a watershed moment in Duchamp, who let in a first breath of fresh air. For us curators these things came to the fore with Harald Szeemann in the 1960s. And suddenly the breath of fresh air became the mainstream. It was the constant reinvention of who has the right to say what is art and what is not. And up until then, all this was liberating and emancipatory. The question now is: what happens when art becomes part of the corridors of power, a massive educational and economic tool, a gentrification tool, a source of entertainment and fun for the family, but also a subtle circulation of ideas explaining how the world works—and how it should work instead. And once we get to there, the question of use is beside the point. It is of use, it is useful. To financial interests, political interests, educational interests, professional interests. There are jobs at stake.

NH

That brings us to institutional practices, and how institutions deal with those conditions. My experiences have been quite varied. I recognize what you describe one hundred percent, certainly from my British experience. I think it's quite different now, working in Belgium, in an institution (M HKA) that I'm grateful is rather forward-thinking and flexible. It bears elements of the situation you describe, but thankfully not entirely, and there are always enough interesting elements that make the whole thing worthwhile. To come to this question of 'use', actually it became a buzzword within the L'Internationale confederation. We made a five-year project called The Uses of Art, and the assignment was to try and understand how art can have some kind of positive societal effect through institutional work. The participant institutions are all rather different, but are like-minded in the sense of talking about use value as opposed to economic value, pure aesthetic value, and do on. I want to take this conversation in the direction of institutional work because I suppose I'm maybe fifty percent with you when it comes to the experience of art in terms of how an audience relates to it. There is certainly an entertainment factor, and there's always a big emphasis on activities, for families, for example. But I would still take an affirmative position in terms of institutions in the public sphere, and in terms of the qualitative level of what institutions are able to do. I know it's not a luxury afforded to everybody; however, I still think it's there. And I would still say that you could differentiate between public institutions and private or market-oriented spaces in terms of motivation, but also in terms of who sets the agenda for driving forward the debates in art. I feel that this is still the case, even if art is still, notionally at least, an avant-garde. But I'm considering how institutions can be a sphere of influence, particularly through the experience of art, because this is where I think institutions underestimate themselves. Because they do have several levels of influence, but often it goes unnoticed. I also think it often takes a very long time and so it's not only the imminence of an individual experience with an artwork or curatorial gesture. I think it's more about long-term impact on society. This is what I'm interested in—how art can become useful on another level.

TZ

You know, this is where it gets more interesting for the readers of this book. When we focus on the fifty percent on which we disagree. Let me clarify that when I say art is put to use for gentrification or entertainment, et cetera, I'm actually not trying to make a moral case. Not for the moment. I'm trying to say that this idea of art simply breaking down barriers, concepts, functionalities, without replacing them with other boundaries and functionalities, is fantasy. In reality, we are always already creating our own audience. The idea of the audience toying with an artwork as an incommensurable experience is just as fantastical. The audiences' interpretations of our work are not that crazy at all. The work itself is packaged with institutional codes that do not encourage any sort of unpredictable, fantastical takes on, you know, flying pigs and pink elephants, and what have you. It's a tightly policed ballgame. And what I wanted to get to is this. Even for people such as Okwui Enwezor, curators you and I looked up to as we entered the field, Maria Lind, Charles Esche, Vasif Kortun—with whom we collaborated on *Lapdogs*—among this closer circle of peers, the good object remains, to use the term of your book, some shade of ambiguity, some form of breaking up. Breaking up clear cut usages and preconceived conventions. When you say 'an influence on society', that's something we would agree on, but most of us see the influence in terms of art as a refusal to distribute new certainties or positions. Undermining the sort of boundaries that were there before. In this role art is always innocent. Suhail would say it has critical virtue. That is the self-image, even if it is not the reality. Does this make sense?

NH

Could you elaborate?

TZ

For example, one of Charles Esche's favourite slogans is, I believe, Spinozan: 'imagining the world differently'. And it's a beautiful phrase, and it dovetails really well with a lot of artistic practices out there. And their political charge. You can see exactly where he's coming from and where he's going with it. But there's a reason why the 'differently' is not pinned down as a programme. That's the crux of the whole thing. The 'difference' has to be held in suspension. And that's possibly the key value that is driving your own project. But maybe you will correct me.

NH

It's a little bit different from that, and this is where I think there's not an incompatibility between what you're talking about and what I'm talking about. I'm talking about ambiguity, and looking at it, certainly aesthetically, but also from an ontological perspective in the context of art. I recently re-read Thierry De Duve's book *Kant after Duchamp*.

You will probably remember how the book opens, with an extra-terrestrial heading to Earth and trying to fathom what artworks are. And then figures from other Earthly fields also try to fathom what art is. For each of them, art is equally baffling. It is somehow its own category of experience and practice. So, I'm on the one hand fascinated by that, whilst conscious that others historically have been critical of the hermeticism of art. However, I'm interested in it in terms of the untapped potential art can bring as a category of experience and a category of practice, in order to have societal influence over time. My reference is the work of psychoanalyst Else Frenkel-Brunswik, who looked at ambiguity in her research. She establishes a direct relation between one's experience of ambiguous stimuli, their cognitive function, and their social outlook. Ambiguity can be encountered in all kinds of things and situations. For example, it can also be with other people—if you encounter someone of ambiguous gender or race for example, and more importantly how you respond on the spectrum of how threatening or desirable you find it. I place art in the rubric of ambiguity, ontologically speaking. But I'm fascinated by the understanding that the more tolerant you are, or can become, of ambiguous experiences, the more imaginative your thought-processes can be, and the more open your social outlook can be as well. I'm excited by this relationship between one's perception, cognitive function, and attitude to society more broadly, and I'm keen to see how this can actually relate to institutional practice. So, I suppose this is the crux of what I'm thinking about. I find inspiration in the fact that actually, ambiguity as part of the artistic experience, can become a driver of institutional work. Ambiguity can in this sense also be determinate and located. This is again why I don't necessarily see a contradiction between your critique of indeterminacy and my understanding of ambiguity. The question then is whether this motivation I identify can be located or not. Does that make sense?

TZ

Totally. I'll try and push back on this located-ness in a minute, but first, two things. One is that I'm with you on the hermeticism. I don't have any problem with that. I don't have any problem with seeing contemporary art as a category of experience which has its distinctive features and strengths and histories. Whether we like or not, it does so, objectively speaking. I don't think there's any point in wishing it was 'sorta' like science or claiming it's 'kinda' like design. It is its own thing. It smells, walks, talks differently. Which also means that there is a specialization at hand, regardless. And this specialization needs to be pinned down a little more clearly than just saying that we have to learn to unlearn. Which is still a key slogan in a lot of art schools.

The troika of ambiguity, tolerance, and open social outlooks, is very much the terrain on which contemporary art likes to situate itself. Once the playing field you demarcate is that of ambiguity, and ambiguity is your good object, then the sky is the limit. Because ambiguity is, by definition, not 'either or'. It's this, as well as, as well as, as well as, but also this, and this. When there's a limit to it, it cannot be genuinely ambiguous. It can only be determinate insofar as it can be liquid, and solid, and gaseous, and dust. That's the beauty of ambiguity. At this point, we need to locate all this professionally. There is a field that values these things. Why? Valuing something is not the same as actually living it. I don't think this category of experience called contemporary art is itself as open or ambiguous as it claims to be. Of course, we are ambiguous in the sense that, you know, language and images and hermeneutics are ambiguous. Human existence is ambiguous. But we're no more ambiguous than others. That's not what sets art apart from other traditions. Would you yourself say this troika is what defines the category of art? Or is it what defines the more interesting artistic practices?

NH

In the sense that I use it, it's not about judgment necessarily. Just to use a really simplistic, perhaps banal example—there would have been a certain point in history, when, say, abstract painting emerges, and in the first instance, people say: what the heck is this? This isn't art. Get it away from here. But given enough time and exposure, the sentiment becomes completely reversed, where people actually now love abstract painting. Abstract Expressionist paintings for example–It's a bit mystical, its experiential, and so on. There are demographics of audiences identified as liking it, and that are even catered for through this kind of artwork. But aside from that, I think the fact that it's eventually accepted and becomes normalized, can also be indicative of broader changes and tolerances in society in the long term. I agree that each of us is no more ambiguous than the other, but not everyone realizes or accepts this, often because they are under defining influence of ideological or spiritual forces. Whereas art, though partially instrumentalized by ideology, is largely secular. This is an important and useful characteristic, and I would like to see how the proliferation of institutions can help people become aware of their ambiguity. I'm interested in ambiguity when it's a stimulus rather than a deferment. I think you're right to say that, in terms of the audience interacting with art, it should not be about some unspecified democratic offer of open-endedness. What I know from my limited knowledge of different analyses is that on the one hand, members of the public don't necessarily know what they like or what they want, that is, until they eventually see it. And secondly, they can be open to the experience of unusual things. I think when they enter an institution, they are mentally prepared specifically for this kind of experience, that maybe they wouldn't have anywhere else. But nonetheless, they indulge. It gives a sort of specificity to an art institution. It's how you deal with that relationship in terms of an institutional position. You mentioned Maria Lind and I think for both of us, she has been a mentor figure, I would say. I'm reminded of a really interesting essay she wrote some years ago called 'This is Going to be Really Funny'.[2] She uses the analogy of delivering a joke, where if before telling a joke, you start by saying 'this is going to be really hilarious', not surprisingly everybody isn't going to find it really hilarious because you've already prepared them for the punchline. And I think she is making a comparison with criticality. So, if you put your cards on the table in advance, the criticality dissipates. I think what she's trying to say is that if you keep this positioning of ambiguity, then actually there

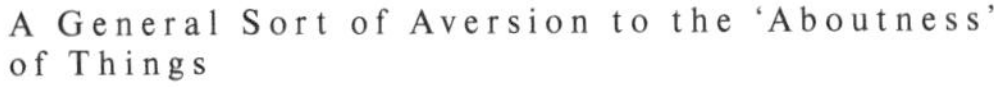

can be a potency to what comes with that. This ought to be translatable to an institutional position.

TZ

Yes, that's a really helpful point. I used to quote that essay a lot. I now find that I disagree with Maria. What she says is spot-on when it comes to humour. I'm not sure it is when it comes to the power and *oomph* and seduction of art. My wager is that you can actually be very blunt. You can be very explicit. You can even explain yourself. And this does not mean, of course, you can do it stupidly. By taking an audience seriously, you can actually provoke something pretty great. One reason why audience reaction has become predictable or conservative is because we don't give them something to clash with. Something to disagree with. A chance to provide an antithesis, a dialectic, which is when something unpredictable happens. Ironically, our fetish for unpredictability, creates predictable reactions again and again. Whereas when there's something didactic and in your face, I find that there's a much bigger variety of responses that come up. I've spent a lot of time in art schools. And there's this dilemma of how much to explain. People are scared of destroying the magic by overthinking it. But Duchamp's pissoir-libraries have been filled with overthought interpretations. And it's only getting weirder. It's a bottomless pit. We can stop worrying about killing the joke with explanations, with didacticism, or what have you.

NH

Well, I suppose I'm wondering why it's an either/or? The fact that exhibitions are often both—didactic and ambiguous—would actually be closer to my experiences of institutional work. And it raises other questions for me too. If everything has to be didactic, then wouldn't you be creating another kind of monoculture? I can totally see that there can be very potent work that is very much about being didactic and getting straight to the point. I would maybe think about someone like Jonas Staal, for example.

TZ

Yes, or Renzo Martens' work is equally didactic.

Yes, I think these two artists are really interesting examples of what you're talking about. And I think they are doing important work that generates some constructive provocations. And it does so even in Jonas Staal's case, it creates actual change. I think about the New World Summit initiative that he organizes, and its collaborative role in helping facilitate a new democratic process in Rojava (West Kurdistan), for example.

TZ

Yes. Renzo Martens' Institute for Human Activities actually acquired land together with plantation workers ...

NH

You're absolutely right. Yes. And coincidentally, they are two of the artists I'm working with for the exhibition I'm organizing on 'monoculture'. Jonas Staal is interested in propaganda studies, which I think is useful because propaganda is a highly influential phenomenon that art can't really compete with on a certain level. Despite the fact that it's also adopting this post-modern attitude of relative truth as a way to generate influence.

TZ

I think our working premise, which we inherited from the post-structuralists, implies there is no point in talking about a reality out there, at least not independently of the concepts we have for grasping it. We're caught within the concepts and language we would use to grasp reality. Reality itself is off limits, the stuff of theologians. Whereas if you were to accept that there is something out there that exists independently of our concepts and language, well then you must try harder to put them to use, to actually do justice to the stuff that is out there. And then propaganda does make sense. But as long as you firmly believe that we're trapped in language, there's no point in that.

NH

But to finish my point: I was on the one hand looking at artists whose work really makes sense in terms of coming

straight towards addressing relevant concerns in a very didactic way. But on the other hand, I also think about, for example, Steve McQueen's *Queen and Country* project from 2007. I'm not particularly interested in the work of McQueen, but this for me made a really interesting case study. You probably remember, he was invited by the Imperial War Museum in London to be an official war artist, and after much cogitation eventually came up with the idea to produce a set of stamps with the portraits of all British soldiers who died in the Iraq War. He wanted them to be produced and distributed by Royal Mail. What was really interesting is that instead of taking a position on the war itself, he deliberately kept his position ambiguous, as to whether he was for or against the war. Actually, this was really important, in terms of the debate and meaning generated around it. People who were against the war wanted to see the stamps published. And, people who were for the war also wanted to see the stamps published. It was vetoed ultimately by the Ministry of Defence. But it could only have had that sort of level of impact because he kept his own position ambiguous. So, for me, this is an interesting case study of when the position of ambiguity can be rather determined in order to have potency.

TZ

Nice dichotomy you set up. And yes, Jonas Staal and Renzo Martens are out there. And there are actually a lot of artists like them. Without going into the conceptual qualities of the one in comparison to the other, they do both fuck with the orthodoxy of contemporary art, and, more importantly, they propose a different one, a different orthodoxy. But the fact remains that they are a minority. For every Renzo Martens you show me, I'll show you fifty Steve McQueens. The ratio is very clear. As for spurring debate. Art can go much further than that. It's not enough to do this critical peekaboo thing. Maybe it was enough in the 1990s, when we thought time was on our side, and that we just had to be critical and aware, and then all those bad things like nationalism and musty old museums and bad patriarchs would go away. But especially when you have people running the show from Brazil to the US to Hungary who disregard boundaries between fact and fiction in a way that would make an artist blush, it's not what is most needed.

NH

I certainly agree with that. I'd be interested to hear your opinion on something, partly because I already have quite a strong opinion on it myself. I want to ask this because you also mentioned Charles Esche, earlier, and I think he's one of the proponents in the tendency of 'decoloniality'. He also uses the word 'demodernize' to talk about institutional practice, which is related. But you might see that decoloniality has become some kind of movement, and a didactic one at that, which is openly trying to cause change. I suppose I also connect it with this term 'moral economy' that you're using. I'd be interested to hear your opinion on that?

TZ

On decoloniality? The energy crystallized around that has sparked important conversations that otherwise would not have materialized. Not sure it has sparked a decisive effect within art, though. With the emphasis on the de-, like as a de-territorializing, de-constructing, un-learning and so forth, it slips very comfortably into the slipstream of this overall moral economy of indeterminacy that I've been describing and which invites us to revisit until we lose sight of what we do. How do you then recolonize? After all this hard labour, how tolerant are you going to be, when it comes to someone's often firm and unironic positions. I'm getting the sense that for every hour we spend analyzing, illustrating, exposing a marginalized condition, we barely spend a moment trying to imagine how to replace that condition with something else. Look, I'd rather there's a discussion around decolonizing than, you know, Abstract Expressionism. I'll take decolonizing any day, but I think that it's really just a first step, like institutional critique. Anyway, that's a whole other discussion. Maybe a bit of a side-track. My brain is melting. Mr. Haq. And home schooling awaits. Mercy.

NH

Typical. Me, I was only getting started. Why do I always

place my faith in you? A pox on you, and your kind, throughout your generations forever.

TZ
Gee, thanks Nav. It's nice to be working with you again.
You haven't changed.

Notes

1 *Lapdogs of the Bourgeoisie: Class Hegemony in Contemporary Art* was a series of exhibitions co-curated by Nav Haq and Tirdad Zolghadr between 2006 and 2009. The exhibitions took place at Gasworks, London (19 November 2006-14 January 2007); Platform Garanti, Istanbul (23 January-3 March 2007); Tensta konsthall, Stockholm (11 January-30 March 2008); Townhouse Gallery, Cairo (9 November-3 December 2008); and Arnolfini, Bristol (2 May-5 July 2009)

2 Maria Lind, 'This Is Going To Be Really Funny: Notes on Art, Its Institutions and their Presumed Criticality', in exh. cat. *Spin Cycle*, ed. Nav Haq (Bristol: Spike Island, 2004), pp. 33-43.

Notes on Blackness, Darkness, and Shadowlands

Paolo S.H. Favero

> Darkness is your candle.
> Rumi

Suddenly the light was gone. It was a few years ago. And there was no one there to guide me. Every point of reference was lost. I was wrapped in the dark. A deep sense of void sucking me back down to mother earth. The desire of not being. The perception of the eye getting in tune with that of the soul. Blackness. 'I go back to black' sang Amy Winehouse amidst her despair.

Instead of fighting it, I chose to enter darkness. And eventually my eyes began to adjust. As they say in the theatre world, darkness does in fact not exist. A dark room, a proper dark room, a space of total invisibility can never be fully created. And in fact, in my darkness too I slowly started seeing again, a different world, a world made up of what no longer was. A world inhabited by the 'ghosts of my life' to quote from the title of Mark Fisher's (2014) wonderful book.

In the midst of my darkness I began to see shapes. I saw my ghosts coming alive. From the past straight into my present they pointed me towards the future. I could see them dancing all around me, in swirls, circles, and spirals. A choreography of present absences accompanying me during my everyday life. Shadows. And suddenly love emerged through these shapes. It appeared to me in the shape of light. The light of possibility. A thin border between what actually is and what could be. 'Prospect' is the word I choose for defining this light, the one that can break through the darkness. Prospect is a word that a friend of mine in Delhi suggested to me. A prospect is something special indeed. It is not a guarantee, it is not a plan. A prospect is just a possibility. Yet one that faithfully points ahead without actually visualizing a clear path. 'Prospect' suits the darkness. It is there in potency, but it cannot really be seen. A prospect represents the clinging on to life and its beauty.

Prospect and possibilities, are, after all, all that human beings have. This is something that those of us trapped in the neoliberal capitalist tsunami tend to forget. Life is an unclear, uncertain continuum filled up as much by darkness as by light. And sometimes it is only the darkness, the blackness that can teach us to see. In the present digitized contexts of the world, the strife for constant visibility (though Instagram, Facebook, etc.) makes us forget that sometimes it is in the spaces of blackness, where it is impossible to see, that light can be perceived. Invisibility is a powerful communicator.

This idea, this inversion, has been at the centre of many philosophies such as Buddhism, Tantrism and Sufism. It is summed up in Persian poet Rumi's suggestion that 'the wound is where the light enters your body'. Within this logic, removal (just like pain and suffering) are just as important for human life as accumulation and pleasure. A strange concept for a capitalist world. In the West, in fact, (whatever this label may stand for) and in the capitalist reigns of the world we are thought to overcome, ignore, or even attack all that we attach to these dark areas. 'We' want to stick to the light, to see and be seen, believing that only in this way we are given access to clarity and knowledge. 'Enlightenment' is after all the core motto of Western civilization.

Yet, the spaces of darkness and blackness and those of suffering, weakness, defeat, and death can show us the way too. In the darkness we can learn to connect life with death, love with hate, pleasure with pain. The Indian philosopher Jiddu Krishnamurti explained this very clearly when he said that death is the ultimate state of enlightenment. That is when humans empty themselves of all their assumptions. And only in this emptiness can they learn to see things clearly. And this is an act of cleansing of the mind. In 1966 Krishnamurti said:

> I wonder how you see things. Do you see them with your eyes, with your mind? Obviously, you see things with your eyes, but you see with the mind much more quickly than with the eye. You see the world much more quickly than the eye can perceive. You see with memory, with knowledge, and when you so see things, that is with the mind, you are seeing what has been, not what actually is.[1]

The relativity of these notions can be visualized also in the different associations that can be found in the world between colour and death. To give a simple binary, while the West addresses death with black, for Hinduism it is white. White is the colour to be worn during funerals and mourning. As we know white is after all the result of the merging of all colours. If you paint a wheel with all colours and let it spin quickly, white is what you will see. All colours merge into it, as they do if you make a long exposure photograph of the sea early in the morning. The deep blue, emerald and

turquoise sea will turn into a foamy white. And indeed, this idea
fits well with the overarching notion of reincarnation. According
to Hinduism, every individual is in fact nothing but a collection
of particles connected to the Universe. The individual spirit (the
purusa) is nothing but part of the broader *Purusa*, the spirit of
cosmos, God. At the end of a human life the spirit is split up
into many different particles that recompose within the universe.
According to this view, the end is therefore always the beginning
of something else. Hence, death is life. Black is white. Darkness is
light. All the elements come together. During an open-air crema-
tion ritual in Delhi I witnessed this merging of colours. And old
man taught me to detect the changing colours of the flame. As the
flame crawls down to the body the colour changes, reacting to the
life of a decaying body. The love for the dead is the love for life. It
all comes down to white ash that, at the end, will be thrown back
into the world by the wind.

So, the possibility is that blackness and darkness can be
seen as more than spaces of absence, negation, danger. And it
quite evident that in the West there has been little attention to the
shifting meanings (and to the lightness) of black. As the history of
cinema has told us, film chemicals were produced to capture the
subtle shades of white skin but never of black skin. The same debate popped up recently also with regard to smartphone cameras
and Instagram filters. So how to enquire deeper into the materiality and ontology of blackness and darkness?

The shadow is probably the best metaphor and phenomenon for entering and exploring this terrain. In the shadowlands
black and white, light and darkness, life and death meet and
merge, they dance with each other, inverting positions and meanings. I want to enter the question of darkness and blackness from
this particular angle. Shadowlands are a space revealing the co-
existence and co-dependence between the opposite extremes that
make up the human experience. Shadows are in fact quintessential
possibilities. They mark that thin boundary between darkness and
light. Between presence and absence. Between black and white.

My interest for shadows developed during the time that I
was caught in the darkness. The one I referred to above. During
this time, I became almost obsessed with observing shadows. I
loved exploring that moment in the late afternoon when nature
attempts to retreat into invisibility. During these moments I could
observe how the electric bulb, the prosthetic prolongation of the

human eye, would gradually take over and dominate the city scape. The effect of the bulb was impressive. Through its presence the single, majestic source of light of the sun would be split up into a plethora of micro-suns. Electricity, I noticed, transformed the city into a new landscape, a world of pluralities and contradictions. Under the light of the street lamp I could witness my own self being split up into its various micro-selves, into many shadows, into its own possibilities and prospects. In the nightly city lights my individual shadow morphed into a multiplicity of shadows; a choreography of shadows dancing and moving all around me as I moved, like the ghosts of my life. In the city lights I became unsure of who I was. Like Peter Pan (see below) I felt that I had lost my shadow and, along with that, my sense of self. Unlike Peter Pan, though, I enjoyed the loss. And if it is true that, as Rabindranath Tagore made us understand, becoming oneself is, as Hanif Qureshi beautifully paraphrased it, something that 'we always do in company', then the shadow is a good indicator of that. Shadows are always in company and the night, with its darkness, is a provider of wisdom.

During that period in my life I also got used to chase shadows in the morning. I wanted to be out on the streets before the city would really come to life. I loved witnessing the moment of the day when the electric light would give way to the sun, again. When the prosthetic-electric would make room for nature again. I loved taking part in that precious, transformative moment when the multiple selves that the night helped scatter around would recompose into one. The multiple shadows of the city lights would slowly recompose themselves into one singular shadow. The sun would invite me to return to my-self, I had to become self again, an in-dividual (another culturally relative notion), neglectful of contradictions, ready for another productive day.

The play of shadows is hence more than an optical matter. It speaks to our vision of the self, to our constant labour of identity-making. Shadows are transformative presences that allow us to discover the other side of our selves. The shadow is the thin membrane that separates us from the world of darkness. Separating day and night, blackness and light, it offers us a renewed way of looking at the world.

Shadows have indeed nurtured the fantasies of writers and artists alike. In Western civilizations the shadow carries somewhat uncanny and most often negative connotations. Shadows are conventionally associated with fear, with notions of danger and loss; they are dark and worrisome. Shadows speak of removal and absence; of superficiality and negative forces. Shadows are proverbial figures that hunt the living and stand for the dark side of life. We therefore speak of 'shadow government' or 'shadow economy', suggesting that the shadow stands for something somewhat mysterious and unethical. 'When small people start casting big shadows it is time for sunset' says the proverb. The shadow also becomes synonymous with the ghost (as in the 'ghost writer') aligning itself with all that is invisible and scary. Like ghosts, shadows are not good things in Western culture. Think of the scary shadows of German Expressionism and of American horror movies. 'The Curse of the Fires and of the Shadows' was the title William Yates gave one of his short stories.

Freud (1919) elaborated on the shadow in his writings on 'the uncanny'. Building upon Otto Rank's work on the multiple connections between shadows, mirrors, guardian spirits, and the figure of the 'double' (the Doppelgänger), he suggested that the shadow after all represented nothing but an on-going struggle between humans and death. The double, like the shadow, he said, enters the experience of human beings at their childhood as an insurance 'against destruction to the ego' or to use Rank's words, an 'energetic denial of the power of death'. Yet, as the child grows up the double takes on a different meaning: from having been an assurance of immortality, he becomes 'the ghastly harbinger of death'.

Regardless of the point of entrance, we plunge again into an association here between shadows, darkness, blackness, and fears. The shadow is the omen of something scary, threatening, and dangerous. As described with the case of Peter Pan and some of the myths mentioned above, in Western fantasies fears of losing the shadow amount to fears of loss of the self. In *Pendulum*, a song about the inevitability of death, the American band Pearl Jam sings 'My shadow left me long ago'.

But in the West shadows are also considered to be the true side of the soul. This can be found in many myths, folk legends, and superstition. 'Don't trust people with no shadow!' says another famous popular maxim. A sense that the shadow is connected to the true side of an individual is hence there in the West too. And it is no coincidence that in that civilization, which is guided by notions of in-dividuality, the shadow is always in singular form.

We have one, not many shadows and we are, unlike in other civilizations, one, and not many selves.

Peter Pan materializes this idea very well. I introduced this above but let me now look deeper into it. In J.M. Barrie's novel, Peter Pan loses his shadow one night while visiting the house of Mrs. Darling. The latter, finding the shadow, treats it as a mundane object. She washes it, dries it, and stores it in a drawer. It will be Wendy, later on, who will try to stitch it back onto Peter's feet, thereby allowing him to reconnect with his other litigious side. In Disney's film, in fact, Peter keeps flying back and forth in a nightly lit room trying to catch his own shadow, thus re-enacting, albeit in reverse, the play that many kids entertain themselves with; trying to run away or jump away from their own shadow. Peter Pan's experience with his shadow can be easily read as a part of his on-going struggle against growing up ('growing up is the beginning of the end' recites the novel), a struggle between his various selves. The shadow in this context can be easily read as the alter ego of normality (the life of a middle-aged man), a tool helping humans to bring their own life into a critical perspective. The shadow is not where we should be. Shadows in fact are ambiguous, at once superficial and deep, true and fake. They are mundane objects that can be washed, dried, and stored in a drawer.

Shadows sum up some qualities that are considered conflictual with Western rationality and moral. In the first place, as anyone can easily observe, a shadow is a pure surface. Shadows skim upon, morph and adapt to whatever they encounter on their path. A shadow is a pure trace without depth and meaning. Like a caress, it does not seek to change what it touches. Kids discover the wonder of shadows that run after them and which they are trying to shake off. Yet they always fail in doing so. The shadow always wins. Like their conscience, the shadow always comes back to them, keeping them in a hold. Like a gaze, a shadow, to paraphrase the Russian theologian Pavel Florensky, 'tenderly caresses and cuddles the surface of the reality that amazed the philosopher' (2011, p. 76). Yet, surfaces are scary in Western culture. Surfaces are the negation of the true depth of human beings, which, from Greek philosophy onwards is meant to reside in the soul, in the inner invisible parts of humans. And the shadow is its total negation, it is pure ephemerality. In her writings on surfaces Barbara Maria Stafford (1996) attacks the 'totemization of language as a godlike agency' that characterizes Western culture.

She suggests that the linguist Ferdinand de Saussure's schema 'emptied the mind of its body' reducing images to 'encrypted messages requiring decipherment' (Stafford 1996, pp. 5–6). Western culture builds on the principle that surfaces are devoid of meaning and substance.

But indeed, the roots of these ideas are to be found further back in time. Through the cave experiment Plato instilled in Western culture the pervasive idea that shadows (and along with them images) are deceivers. They negate truth and knowledge, subjugating human beings to false myths. This notion got indeed reinforced by Descartes' hierarchization between body and mind. His vision of the senses as part of the fallible human body and of the intellect (which according to him was connected to the soul) as the ultimate 'interpreting judge of sensory perception' (cf. Mirzoeff 1999, p. 43), further highlighted this distinction.

A second dimension of shadows that is worth addressing is that they are also somewhat contradictory. While being a physical object, a phenomenological fact, they are indeed also deprived of materiality. Shadows do exist but they cannot be touched, grabbed, directed (this is where the defying force in Peter Pan lies). As such they are a part of our life-world, of our experiences but in a very uncomfortable, troubling way. We are never sure how to approach them and what to do with them. And this problem has grown even stronger given the many transformation that shadows, as ontological things, have been exposed to through human intervention (with the discovery of first fire and later the invention of electricity). At the most basic level, shadows are always in motion but tend to appear to us, as a result of the interaction of physical bodies with the light of the sun, as fairly stable. Yet, in the presence of fire, or of a candle, they at once show their dynamic nature. Shadows flicker, achieving a capacity to animate themselves, to move and make the environment around them change accordingly. Even more so, in the presence of electric light (as I discussed above) shadows become uncanny figures, multiplying their presence in our life-worlds. Shadows populate our cities and our mundane urban experience of the night. Sometimes they anticipate our movements, sometimes they guard us from behind. At the end of every day, as the 'natural' shadow abandons us, the artificial ones (note the plural form) come to the fore. If shadows are, as myths would have it, an emanation of our true self, then our self is a multiplicity, split into parts. When primitive people learned to produce light by means of fire, they also managed to craft their own artificial shadows, filling up the gap created by that big shadow that we call the night. After all, the night too is nothing but one big shadow created by the constant interplay between the Sun and the Earth.

Shadows seem to constitute a threat against key pillars of Western thought and science, with their fascination for dualisms, for clear-cut lines, for linear narrations and separations (something that runs as a continuum from Descartes to Renaissance perspective and the construction of nation states, from Christian cosmology to the fundaments of Capitalist ideology). Porous, ephemeral, ever-changing, immaterial, ungraspable, shadows challenge dualisms and separations. Where exactly does the line between light and dark run in a shadow? Where does the shadow begin and where does it end?

Moving in space and time we cannot but notice the extent to which shadows have been addressed by other civilizations in a more propositive manner helping us realize that, paraphrasing Roberto Casati (2004), shadows not only hide, they also reveal. The propositive, productive aspect embedded in a shadow can, for instance, be detected in the invention of the sundial, which reads the time of day on the basis of the shadow projected by the sun on a stick. Shadows are also useful for characterizing space. To give one example, author Hans Ruesch (1977) called the land in which the Inuits lived 'the land of long shadows'. Defining the unicity of the long sundown and dawn that can be found in the northern part of the Northern hemisphere, over time this term was adopted for describing all lands of the North.

Shadows are also at the core of the invention of photography (the first images produced were shadows imprinted on paper or metal plates). And even before that, they were used to make portraits through the famous method of the silhouette (the precursor of modern visual identification methods). And they were also deployed extensively for entertainment purposes with the shadow theatres, which are still popular in many parts of Asia (and not only there). Moving back in time, the Romans too consciously incorporated the use of shadows for the construction of immersive environments, using them to blur the distance between the physical word and the world as it was perceived by humans. In the Ara Pacis Augustae (Altar of Augustan Peace) in Rome, for instance, internal space is shaped through a merging of bas-relief (depicting scenes from mythology) and elements of nature (mainly leaves) inserted in and on the walls. Here, shadows are fundamental to the creation of a sense of depth that confuses the viewers with regard to their position in space. Imagining, as art historian Giulio Argan described it, the wall not 'as a solid surface, but as a spatiality or imaginary depth' (2008, p. 147) the Romans exploited the shadows to act upon the perception of physical space.

Shadows do have a capacity to blur our conventional experience of space. Think of how the projection of the shadow of a tree can gently fall upon, and merge with, the sleek marble surface of a modern building or a monument. They can help bring the human-made environment and nature in contact with each other.

Just like love, shadows are generous and have an immense capacity to accumulate and overlap. 'Two shadows can occupy the same space without bothering one another', says Casati (p. 41). The shadow is like love, like transcendental love, always capable of more.

We have however to remain in the Eastern parts of the world to really acknowledge the generative capacity of shadows. The dialectic between darkness and light is what characterizes the design and architecture of many Sufi mausolea. Visiting, for instance, the tomb of Ghalib and of other historical figures in Nizammuddin, the Sufi Islamic neighbourhood in South Delhi (India), the passing of time causes a continuous movement of light across the beautiful marble grids that decorate the walls surrounding the tombs. In the absence of a human representation of God—in Sufism, as in all Islam, God, who is also metaphorized by means of the word Love, can never be visually portrayed—God enters the space of the living in the shape of a play between shadow and light. Here the shadow highlights the role of light, just like in Rumi's poems. It uses the principle of inversion. I realized this dialectic more than ever a few months ago when I was observing a cat playing with shadows. A female kitten, Vilma (that is her name) was running in all directions, almost possessed by the shapes projected on the floor through the hands and objects waved by the people around her. And indeed, what Vilma was following was the light, not the shadow. The latter only helped to create room for the light to be properly engaged with and enjoyed.

Like many other Sufi poets, the thirteenth-century Persian poet Rumi often referred to the notion of the shadow in his writings. For him, the shadow (and darkness) was, however, never a matter of absence, the loss of something (of light, vision, understanding). On the contrary, it was the very essence that made humans appreciate the true meaning of light, visions, and knowledge, in other words of Life and of Love and hence of God. In an inversion typical for much Sufi poetry and art, Rumi wrote that 'You must have shadow and light source both' and that 'both light and shadow are the dance of Love ... Lover and loving are inseparable and timeless'. In his poem *Wetness and Water* he wrote:

> *How does*
> *A part of the world*
> *Leave the world?*
>
> *How does wetness*
> *Leave water?*
>
> *Don't try to put out fire*
> *By throwing on more fire!*
>
> *Don't wash a wound*
> *With blood.*
>
> *No matter how fast you run,*
> *Your shadow keeps up.*
>
> *Only full, overhead sun*
> *diminishes your shadow.*
>
> *But that shadow has been serving you.*
> *What hurts you blesses you.*
>
> *Darkness is your candle.*
> *Your boundaries are your quest*

1 The quote is taken from a public talk held in 1966 in Saanen, www.journal.kfionline.org/issue-9/silent-looking-exploring-perceptionwith-j-krishnamurti.

References

— Argan, Giulio C. 2008. *Storia dell'arte italiana: Dall'Antichità al Medioevo*. Milan: RCS Libri.
— Casati, Roberto. 2004. *Shadows: Unlocking Their Secrets, from Plato to Our Time*. London: Vintage.
— Fisher, Mark. 2014. *Ghosts of My Life: Writings on Depression, Hauntology and Lost Futures*. London: Zero Books.
— Florensky, Pavel A. 2011. *Stupore e dialettica*. Macerata: Quodlibet.
— Freud, Sigmund. 1919, *The 'Uncanny' Imago*. Available online: https://web.mit.edu/allanmc/www/freud1.pdf (accessed 16 February, 2019).
— Mirzoeff, Nicholas. 1999. *An Introduction to Visual Culture*. London: Routledge.
— Ruesch, Hans. 1977. *Back to the Top of the World*. London: Pocket.
— Stafford, Barbara M. 1996. *Good Looking. Essays on the Virtue of Images*. Cambridge, MA: The MIT Press.

Contributors

Paolo S.H. Favero (1969) is Associate Professor in Film Studies and Visual Culture at the Dept. of Communication Studies, University of Antwerp, where he is also a member of the Visual and Digital Cultures Research Centre (ViDi). He chairs the MA in Film Studies and Visual Culture at the University of Antwerp, co-convenes the Visual Anthropology Network of EASA (the VANEASA) and is the vice-chair of the ECREA section for Visual Cultures. A visual anthropologist trained at Stockholm University, Favero has devoted the core of his career to the study of visual culture in India and to the use of emerging digital visual technologies at the methodological level. Presently he conducts research on ageing, dying, and time in India. He is the author of the *The Present Image: Visible Stories in a Digital Habitat* (2018) and of *Image-Making-India: Visual Culture, Technology, Politics* (forthcoming).

Pascal Gielen (1970) is professor of sociology of culture and politics at the Antwerp Research Institute for the Arts (Antwerp University) where he leads the Culture Commons Quest Office (CCQO). Gielen is editor of the international book series Antennae—Arts in Society (Valiz). In 2016 he became laureate of the Odysseus grant for excellent international scientific research of the Fund for Scientific Research Flanders in Belgium. Gielen has published many books which are translated in Chinese, English, Polish, Portuguese, Russian, Spanish, Turkish, and Ukrainian. His research focuses on creative labour, the commons, and urban and cultural politics. Gielen works and lives in Antwerp, Belgium.

Christine Greiner (1961) is professor of Politics and Arts of the Body at the Graduate Programme of Communication and Semiotics (Pontifical Catholic University of São Paulo) where she leads the Centre for Oriental Studies (CEOr). Greiner is the author of several books, including *The Body: Clues for Interdisciplinary Studies* (2005), *The Body in Crisis: Short-circuit of Representations* (2010), *Readings of the Body in Japan and Cognitive Diasporas* (2015), and *Fabulations of the Japanese Body and Microactivisms* (2017). She was a visiting professor at Paris VIII, Kansai Gaidai (International Programme), and Rikkyo University; and a visiting researcher at the Performance Studies Department of Tisch School of the Arts in New York, Center Nichibunken of Kyoto, among others. Greiner works and lives in São Paulo, Brazil.

Max Haiven is Canada Research Chair in Culture, Media and Social Justice at Lakehead University in Northwest Ontario and director of the ReImagining Value Action Lab (RiVAL). He writes articles for both academic and general audiences and is the author of the books *Crises of Imagination, Crises of Power: Capitalism, Creativity and the Commons* (2014), *The Radical Imagination: Social Movement Research in the Age of Austerity* (with Alex Khasnabish, 2014) and *Cultures of Financialization: Fictitious Capital in Popular Culture and Everyday Life* (2014). His latest book, *Art after Money, Money after Art: Creative Strategies Against Financialization*, was published by Pluto in Fall 2018. His book *Revenge Capitalism: The Ghosts of Empire, the Demons of Capital, and the Settling of Unpayable Debts* will appear in 2020.

Nav Haq (1976) is Associate Director at M HKA, responsible for the development of its artistic programme. He was previously Exhibitions Curator at Arnolfini, Bristol (2007–2012) and Curator at Gasworks, London (2004–2007).

Haq has organized numerous monographic exhibitions with artists such as Cosima von Bonin, Shilpa Gupta, Imogen Stidworthy, Harald Thys & Jos de Gruyter, and Otobong Nkanga, as well as significant overviews of work by Hüseyin Bahri Alptekin, Joseph Beuys, Kerry James Marshall, and Laure Prouvost. Haq was curator of the 2017 edition of the Göteborg International Biennial of Contemporary Art and Contour Biennial 2007, Mechelen, Belgium. At M HKA he co-curated the group exhibition *Don't You Know Who I Am? Art After Identity Politics* in 2014, and curated the interdisciplinary exhibition *Energy Flash: The Rave Movement*. Haq is on the editorial board of the online research platform for the L'Internationale confederation of European museums. In 2012, he was recipient of the Independent Vision Award for Curatorial Achievement, awarded by Independent Curators International, New York.

Hedwig Houben (1983) lives and works in Brussels. She studied at AKV|St.Joost in Breda (2002-2006), Kunstakademie Düsseldorf (2006–2007), and the Flanders Higher Institute for Fine Arts/HISK (2010-2011). Houben's artworks consider our relationship to objects, particularly how we live with them, and how they might play a role in the formation of our selfhood. Her previous solo exhibitions include: *SWEEP, TAP, SWOOOOOP*, M HKA, Antwerp (2019), *You and I*, Spike Island, Bristol (2016) and *The Hand, the Eye and It*, 1646, The Hague (2013). Her work has been on display in a variety of group exhibitions, including Lofoten Biennial (2015), *Un-Scene*, Wiels, Brussels (2015), *Don't You Know Who I Am? Art After Identity Politics*, M HKA, Antwerp (2014), and *Six Possibilities for a Sculpture*, La Loge, Brussels (2013).

Iman Issa
Iman Issa (1979) is an artist, and professor at the Academy of Fine Arts in Vienna. Recent solo and group exhibitions include Hamburger Bahnhof, Berlin, MoMA, New York, the Solomon R. Guggenheim Museum, New York, 21er Haus, Vienna, MACBA, Barcelona, the Perez Art Museum, Miami, New Museum, New York, KW Institute of Contemporary Art, Berlin, the 12th Sharjah Biennial, and the 8th Berlin Biennale. Books include *Book of Facts: A Proposition* (2017), *Common Elements* (2015) and *Thirty-three Stories about Reasonable Characters*

in Familiar Places (2011). She has been named a 2017 DAAD artist-in-residence, and is a recipient of the Vilcek Prize for Creative Promise (2017), the Louis Comfort Tiffany Foundation Award (2015), HNF-MACBA Award (2012), and the Abraaj Group Art Prize (2013).

Bojana Piškur graduated in art history from the University of Ljubljana and received her PhD at the Institute for Art History at the Charles University in Prague, the Czech Republic. She works as a senior curator in the Moderna galerija/Museum of Modern Art in Ljubljana. The focus of her professional interest is on political issues as they relate to or are manifested in the field of art, with special emphasis on the region of (former) Yugoslavia. She has curated, written for numerous publications and lectured in many parts of the world on topics such as post avant-gardes in Yugoslavia, radical education, socialist cultural politics and the Non-Aligned Movement. Her recent exhibition that dealt with the topic of the non-alignment was *Southern Constellations: The Poetics of the Non-Aligned*, Moderna galerija Ljubljana (2019).

Public Movement is a performative research body that investigates and stages political actions in public spaces. It studies and creates public choreographies, forms of social order, overt and covert rituals. Recent exhibitions include Guggenheim Museum (New York), Tel Aviv Museum of Art (Tel Aviv), Vistamarestudio gallery (Milan). In 2017, Public Movement won the Rosenblum Prize for Performing Arts, and in 2014 they were shortlisted for the Future Generation Art Prize at the Pinchuk Art Centre, Kiev. In 2015, Alhena Katsof and Dana Yahalomi wrote *Solution 263: Double Agent*, published by Sternberg Press. The group performed in the Asian Art Biennial, Taipei; Novecento Museum, Florence; Steirischer Herbst Festival, Graz; Berlin Biennial; New Museum Triennial, New York; Performa, New York; Gothenburg Biennial, Van Abbemuseum, Eindhoven; MAXXI, Rome and more. Public Movement was founded in Tel Aviv, Israel on 29 December 2006 by Dana Yahalomi and Omer Krieger. Yahalomi became the sole director of the group in 2011.

Jonas Staal (1981) is a visual artist whose work deals with the relation between art, propaganda, and democracy. He is the founder of the organization New World Summit (2012–ongoing) and with Florian Malzacher he is currently directing the utopian training camp Training for the Future (2018-ongoing). Exhibition-projects include *Art of the Stateless State* (Moderna galerija, Ljubljana, 2015), *The Scottish-European Parliament* (CCA, Glasgow, 2018) and *Museum as Parliament* (Van Abbemuseum, Eindhoven, 2018–ongoing). His projects have been exhibited widely at venues such as the Stedelijk Museum in Amsterdam and Moderna Museet in Stockholm, as well as the 7th Berlin Biennale (2012), the 31st São Paulo Biennale (2014), The Oslo Architecture Triennale (2016) and the Warsaw Biennale (2019). His most recent publication is *Propaganda Art in the 21st Century* (MIT Press, 2019). Staal completed his PhD research on propaganda art at the PhDArts programme of Leiden University, the Netherlands.

Mi You is a lecturer at the Academy of Media Arts Cologne. Her long-term research and curatorial projects spin between the two extremes of the ancient and the futuristic. She works with the Silk Road as a figuration for nomadic imageries and old and new networks/technologies. She has curated programmes at Asian Culture Centre in Gwangju, South Korea, Ulaanbaatar International Media Art Festival, Mongolia (2016), and with Binna Choi she is co-steering a research/curatorial project *Unmapping Eurasia*. At the same time, her interests in politics around technology and futures led her to work on 'actionable speculations', articulated in the exhibition, workshops and sci-fi-a-thon *Sci-(no)-fi* at the Academy of the Arts of the World, Cologne (2019), as well as in her function as chair of committee on Media Arts and Technology for the transnational political NGO Common Action Forum. She is one of the curators of the 13th Shanghai Biennale (2020-2021)

Tirdad Zolghadr (1973) is a curator and writer. He is currently artistic director of the Sommerakademie Paul Klee in Bern, Switzerland. Curatorial work includes biennial settings as well as long-term, research-driven efforts, most recently as associate curator at KW Institute for Contemporary Art Berlin, 2016–2020. Theoretical writing includes *Traction*, Sternberg Press 2016. Ongoing work on Zolghadr's third novel, *Headbanger*, is made possible thanks to generous support by the Foundation for Arts Initiatives.

M HKA

This publication has been produced to coincide with the exhibition:

MONOCULTURE
A Recent History
M HKA – Museum of Contemporary Art Antwerp
25 September 2020 – 24 Janaury 2021

M HKA TEAM
General and Artistic Director: Bart De Baere
Managing Director: Dieter Vankeirsbilck
Associate Director: Nav Haq
Team: Jürgen Addiers, Jamaheer Jaafar Al-Kadhimi, Fadil Ayoujil, Olcay Bakir, Katrien Batens, Lotte Beckwé, Giulia Bellinetti, Evi Bert, Maya Beyns, Leen Bosch, Els Brans, Josine Buggenhout, Veerle Bydekerke, Tom Ceelen, Ann Ceulemans, Riyad Cherif Chaker, Celina Claeys, Christophe Clarijs, Christine Clinckx, Leen De Backer, Annelien De Troij, Bert De Vlegelaer, Jan De Vree, Martine Delzenne, Liliane Dewachter, Kunchok Dhondup, Dirk Dumoulin, Lode Geens, Marco Harmsen, Abdelhouahed Hasnaoui, Sabine Herrygers, Goele Jacquemyn, Joris Kestens, Nico Köppe, Danny Kortleven, Renild Krols, Christine Lambrechts, Hughe Lanoote, Viviane Liekens, Erik Martens, Natalie Meeusen, Lotte Ogiers, Ilse Raps, Marleen Reijmen, Gabriëla Rib, Anne-Claire Schmitz, Anja Isabel Schneider, Chris Straetling, Jan Stuyck, Georges Uittenhout, Jos Van den Bergh, Ria Van den Broeck, Sarah van Hapert, Chantal Van Hauter, Piet Van Hecke, Kaat Vannieuwenhuyse, Roel Van Nunen, Gerda Van Paemele, Lutgarde Van Renterghem, Marjon Van Waelvelde, Madiken Verboven, Orlando Verde, Els Verhaegen, Ekaterina Vorontsova, Lot Wens, Hans Willemse, Abdel Ziani, Joanna Zielińska
Intern: Marlies Hamal

M HKA BOARD
President: Herman De Bode
Vice-President: Yolande Avontroodt
Board Members: Koen Derkinderen, Annick Garmyn, Vasif Kortun, Katrien Mattelaer, Jan Rombouts, Frederik Swennen, Eugene Tan, Annelies Thoelen, Toon Wassenberg

Representative of the Flemish Minister of Culture:
Kristina Houthuys
Representative of the Flemish Minister of Finance and Budget:
Karin Heremans

M HKA - Museum of Contemporary Art Antwerp - is an initiative of the Flemish Community and is supported by the City of Antwerp, Allen & Overy, De Standaard, De Olifant, Duvel Moortgat, H ART, Hiscox Insurance, Klara, Leopold Hotel Antwerp, McKinsey & Company, Vooruitzicht

M HKA - Museum of Contemporary Art Antwerp
Leuvenstraat 32
2000 Antwerp
Belgium
www.muhka.be
+32 (0)3 260 99 99

M HKA

L'Internationale

The book *The Aesthetics of Ambiguity: Understanding and Addressing Monoculture* is presented in the framework of 'Our Many Europes', a four-year EU funded programme organized by the museum confederation L'Internationale.

About the L'Internationale Confederation

L'Internationale is a confederation of seven modern and contemporary art institutions. L'Internationale proposes a space for art within a non-hierarchical and decentralized internationalism, based on the values of difference and horizontal exchange among a constellation of cultural agents, locally rooted and globally connected. It brings together seven major European art institutions: Moderna galerija (MG+MSUM, Ljubljana, Slovenia); Museo Nacional Centro de Arte Reina Sofía (MNCARS, Madrid, Spain); Museu d'Art Contemporani de Barcelona (MACBA, Barcelona, Spain); Muzeum Sztuki Nowoczesnej w Warszawie (MSN, Warsaw, Poland); Museum van Hedendaagse Kunst Antwerpen (M HKA, Antwerp, Belgium); SALT (Istanbul and Ankara, Turkey) and Van Abbemuseum (VAM, Eindhoven, the Netherlands), and its partners are HDK-Valand Academy (Gothenburg, Sweden) and the National College of Art and Design (NCAD, Dublin, Ireland).

About 'Our Many Europes'

'Our Many Europes' is a four-year programme (2018–2022) comprising exhibitions, public programming, heritage exchange and institutional experimentation across the Internationale confederation. The programme takes the 1990s as a starting point when our current Europe was born. It aims to think speculatively about the role of culture as a driving force in showing who and how we are in the world.

This project has been funded with support from the European Commission. This publication reflects the views of the authors, and the Commission cannot be held responsible for any use which may be made of the information contained herein.

Index

Young, Irin Marion 22, 24, 31

Z

Zecha, Cecilia Ma 155
Zhao, Tingyang 156
Ziegler, Adolf 54
Žižek, Slavoj 148
Zolghadr, Tirdad 15, 16, 178–181, 183–185, 188–193
Zupančič, Alenka 171, 175

Colophon

Colophon

The Aesthetics of Ambiguity
*Understanding and Addressing
Monoculture*

Editor
Pascal Gielen & Nav Haq

Contributors
Paolo S.H. Favero
Pascal Gielen
Christine Greiner
Max Haiven
Nav Haq
Hedwig Houben
Iman Issa
Bojana Piškur
Public Movement
Jonas Staal
Mi You
Tirdad Zolghadr

Antennae-Arts *in* Society Series N° 29
by Valiz, Amsterdam

Translation
Leo Reijnen

Copy Editing
Leo Reijnen

Proofreading
Els Brinkman

Index
Elke Stevens

Design
Metahaven

Paper Inside
Munken Print 100 gr 1.5

Paper Cover
Bioset 240 gr

Printing and Binding
Wilco, Amersfoort/Meppel

Publisher
Valiz, Amsterdam, 2020
www.valiz.nl

ISBN 978-94-92095-76-3

This publication was made possible
through the generous support of:

ARIA
Antwerp Research Institute for the Arts
University of Antwerp

Antwerp Research Institute for the
Arts, Antwerp University, Antwerp

M HKA

Museum of Contemporary Art
Antwerp

L'internationale   OUR MANY EUROPES

L'Internationale

Antennae-Arts in Society Series
Antennae-Arts in Society is a peer-
reviewed book series that validates
artistic, critical, speculative and
essayistic writing as a full academic
publishing method. Contributions
to the series look up-on the arts as
'antennae', feelers for the cultural
interpretation and articulation of
topical political, economic, social,
technological or environmental
issues.
     The books in this series bring
together audiences of diverse
backgrounds: artists and other
creative makers, academics and
researchers from various disciplines,
critics, writers, journalists,
politicians, curators, and institutional
parties, who wish to broaden their
view in different political, social and
other contexts.
Proposals for book concepts in all
artistic and scientific disciplines
that take culture as the base of
interpretation for the social fabric of
our contemporary lives are welcomed
and will be considered for publication
by the academic board.

*Editorial board Valiz-Arts in Society
book series*:
• Pascal Gielen, Professor of
  Sociology of Culture & Politics,
  at the Antwerp Research Institute
  for the Arts (Antwerp University—
  Belgium), also leads the Culture
  Commons Quest Office (CCQO)
• Thijs Lijster, Assistant Professor in
  the Philosophy of Art and Culture
  at the University of Groningen, and
  researcher
  at the Culture Commons Quest
  Office of the University of Antwerp
• Astrid Vorstermans, Publisher
  Valiz

The authors and the publisher have made every effort to secure permission to reproduce the listed material, illustrations and photographs. We apologise for any inadvert errors or omissions. Parties who nevertheless believe they can claim specific legal rights are invited to contact the publisher.

Distribution:
USA/Canada/Latin America: D.A.P., www.artbook.com
GB/IE: Anagram Books, www.anagrambooks.com
NL/BE/LU: Centraal Boekhuis, www.cb.nl
Europe/Asia: Idea Books, www.ideabooks.nl
Australia: Perimeter Books, www.perimeterdistribution.com

ISBN 978-94-92095-76-3

Printed and bound in the Netherlands

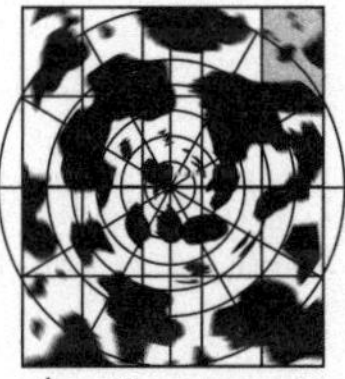

Antennae Series

Antennae N° 1
The Fall of the Studio
Artists at Work
edited by Wouter Davidts & Kim Paice
Amsterdam: Valiz, 2009
(2nd ed.: 2010),
ISBN 978-90-78088-29-5

Antennae N° 2
Take Place
Photography and Place
from Multiple Perspectives
edited by Helen Westgeest
Amsterdam: Valiz, 2009,
ISBN 978-90-78088-35-6

Antennae N° 3
The Murmuring of the
Artistic Multitude
Global Art, Memory and Post-Fordism
Pascal Gielen (author)
Arts *in* Society
Amsterdam: Valiz, 2009
(2nd ed.: 2011),
ISBN 978-90-78088-34-9

Antennae N° 4
Locating the Producers
Durational Approaches to Public Art
edited by Paul O'Neill & Claire
Doherty
Amsterdam: Valiz, 2011,
ISBN 978-90-78088-51-6

Antennae N° 5
Community Art
The Politics of Trespassing
edited by Paul De Bruyne &
Pascal Gielen
Arts *in* Society
Amsterdam: Valiz, 2011 (2nd ed.: 2013),
ISBN 978-90-78088-50-9

Antennae N° 6
See it Again, Say it Again
The Artist as Researcher
edited by Janneke Wesseling
Amsterdam: Valiz, 2011,
ISBN 978-90-78088-53-0

Antennae N° 7
Teaching Art in the
Neoliberal Realm
Realism versus Cynicism
edited by Pascal Gielen &
Paul De Bruyne
Arts *in* Society
Amsterdam: Valiz, 2012
(2nd ed.: 2013),
ISBN 978-90-78088-57-8

Antennae N° 8
Institutional Attitudes
Instituting Art in a Flat World
edited by Pascal Gielen
Arts *in* Society
Amsterdam: Valiz, 2013,
ISBN 978-90-78088-68-4

Antennae N° 9
Dread
The Dizziness of Freedom
edited by Juha van 't Zelfde
Amsterdam: Valiz, 2013,
ISBN 978-90-78088-81-3

Antennae N° 10
Participation Is Risky
Approaches to Joint Creative Processes
edited by Liesbeth Huybrechts
Amsterdam: Valiz, 2014,
ISBN 978-90-78088-77-6

Antennae N° 11
The Ethics of Art
Ecological Turns in the Performing Arts
edited by Guy Cools & Pascal Gielen
Arts *in* Society
Amsterdam: Valiz, 2014,
ISBN 978-90-78088-87-5

Antennae N° 12
Alternative Mainstream
Making Choices in Pop Music
Gert Keunen (author)
Arts *in* Society
Amsterdam: Valiz, 2014,
ISBN 978-90-78088-95-0

Antennae N° 13
The Murmuring of the Artistic
Global Art, Politics and Post-Fordism
Pascal Gielen (author)
Completely revised and enlarged
edition of Antennae N° 3
Arts *in* Society
Amsterdam: Valiz, 2015,
ISBN 978-94-92095-04-6

Antennae N° 14
Aesthetic Justice
Intersecting Artistic and Moral Perspectives
edited by Pascal Gielen &
Niels Van Tomme
Arts *in* Society
Amsterdam: Valiz, 2015,
ISBN 978-90-78088-86-8

Antennae N° 15
No Culture, No Europe
On the Foundation of Politics
edited by Pascal Gielen
Arts *in* Society
Amsterdam: Valiz, 2015,
ISBN 978-94-92095-03-9

Antennae N° 16
Arts Education Beyond Art
Teaching Art in Times of Change
edited by Barend van Heusden &
Pascal Gielen
Arts *in* Society
Amsterdam: Valiz, 2015,
ISBN 978-90-78088-85-1

Antennae N° 17
Mobile Autonomy
Exercises in Artists' Self-Organization
edited by Nico Dockx & Pascal
Gielen
Arts *in* Society
Amsterdam: Valiz, 2015,
ISBN 978-94-92095-10-7

Antennae N° 18
Moving Together
*Theorizing and Making
Contemporary Dance*
Rudi Laermans (author)
Arts *in* Society
Amsterdam: Valiz, 2015,
ISBN 978-90-78088-52-3

Antennae N° 19
Spaces for Criticism
Shifts in Contemporary Art Discourses
edited by Thijs Lijster, Suzana
Milevska, Pascal Gielen,
Ruth Sonderegger
Arts *in* Society
Amsterdam: Valiz, 2015,
ISBN 978-90-78088-75-2

Antennae N° 20
Interrupting the City
Artistic Constitutions of the Public Sphere
edited by Sander Bax, Pascal Gielen
& Bram Ieven
Arts *in* Society
Amsterdam: Valiz, 2015,
ISBN 978-94-92095-02-2

Antennae N° 21
In-between Dance Cultures
*On the Migratory Artistic Identity of
Sidi Larbi Cherkaoui and Akram Khan*
Guy Cools (author)
Arts *in* Society
Amsterdam: Valiz, 2015,
ISBN 978-94-92095-11-4

Antennae N° 22
Imaginative Bodies
Dialogues in Performance Practices
Guy Cools (author)
Arts *in* Society
Amsterdam: Valiz, 2016,
ISBN 978-94-92095-20-6

Antennae N° 23
The Practice of Dramaturgy
Working on Actions in Performance
edited by Konstantina Georgelou,
Efrosini Protopapa,
Danae Theodoridou
Arts *in* Society
Amsterdam: Valiz, 2017,
ISBN: 978-94-92095-18-3

Antennae N° 24
The Art of Civil Action
Political Space and Cultural Dissent
edited by Philipp Dietachmair,
Pascal Gielen
Arts *in* Society
Amsterdam: Valiz, 2017,
ISBN: 978-94-92095-39-8

Antennae N° 25
Commonism
A New Aesthetics of the Real
Nico Dockx & Pascal Gielen
Arts *in* Society
Amsterdam: Valiz, 2018,
ISBN 978-94-92095-47-3

Colophon

Antennae N° 26
The Future of the New
*Artistic Innovation in Times
of Social Acceleration*
Thijs Lijster (ed.)
Arts *in* Society
Amsterdam: Valiz, 2018,
ISBN 978-94-92095-58-9

Antennae N° 27
Contemporary Artist Residencies
Reclaiming Time and Space
edited by Taru Elfving, Pascal Gielen,
Irmeli Kokko
Arts *in* Society
Amsterdam: Valiz, 2019,
ISBN 978-94-92095-46-6

Antennae N° 28
When Fact Is Fiction
Documentary Art in the Post-Truth Era
edited by Nele Wynants
Arts *in* Society
Amsterdam: Valiz, 2020,
ISBN 978-94-92095-71-8